Pest Control for the Smallholder

Pest Control for the Smallholder

David Bezzant

THE CROWOOD PRESS

First published in 2013 by
The Crowood Press Ltd
Ramsbury, Marlborough
Wiltshire SN8 2HR

www.crowood.com

British Library Cataloguing-in-Publication Data
A catalogue record for this book is available from the British Library.

ISBN 978 1 84797 456 3

Acknowledgements
The author would like to acknowledge with gratitude the following for their
co-operation in the preparation of this book: Claire McDermid of STV International,
Richard Allum of Grandpa's Feeders and Mrs Bernie Landshoff of the Domestic
Fowl Trust.

Picture Credits
All pictures are by the author, except where otherwise credited.
Frontispiece: two Fenn traps used for dispatching rats.

Disclaimer
Traps, air rifles, poisons and all equipment and substances used in pest control
should be used in strict accordance with both the law and the manufacturer's
instructions. The author and the publisher do not accept any responsibility in any
manner whatsoever for any error or omission, or any loss, damage, injury, adverse
outcome, or liability of any kind incurred as a result of the use of any of the
information contained in this book, or reliance upon it. If in doubt about any aspect
of pest control readers are advised to seek professional advice.

Typeset by Bookcraft Ltd, Stroud, Gloucestershire
Printed and bound in India by Replika Press Pvt Ltd

Contents

chapter one

The Importance of Pest Control for the Smallholder

INTRODUCTION

I had not been a smallholder for long when I was introduced to the task of pest control. In typical opportunistic fashion, rats were squatting under my chicken shed, which was a relic of post-war Britain and in places susceptible to the gnawing habit of rodents. On hearing of my trouble with these four-legged trespassers a nearby neighbour, who was a wise old countryman with a crumpled face, came to offer advice and presented me with a large tablespoon. I was slightly taken aback until he explained that it was for dispensing poison. When I explained to him that I wanted to use ferrets to deal with the rats he hastily headed home, promising to return with an antiquarian book which contained detailed information on how to mobilize my ferrets against the rats.

With the precious laying hens locked safely out of harm's way, I nervously put my ferret's nose in the mouth of the rat digging leading under the shed. Being fully aware that rats make fierce antagonists, I wondered whether they might make a stand and give my ferret a mauling. My worries were short-lived however, for no sooner had the ferret disappeared than the rats fled at great speed from their hideaway into the path of a waiting terrier.

The ferret has a proven record of dealing with rodents.

Working terriers are instinctive pest catchers and will earn their keep on any smallholding.

This was the beginning of my amateur pest control apprenticeship, which has continued for twenty-five years. One of the first things that struck me was that I was practising an activity that is as old as time itself. Ever since man began to produce food by the cultivation of land and the keeping of livestock, he has had to deal with the undesired attention of animals which, in the process of securing their own comfort and satisfying their own appetites at man's expense, earned the title of 'vermin' and later 'pest'.

Successive generations from every country in the world had to find a way to deal with pests, which were, in some cases, even capable of threatening human life. Accounts of the destructive habits of pests appear in books ranging from the Bible, to the chronicles of American pioneers. In the latter case, Laura Ingalls Wilder, author of the acclaimed *Little House on the Prairie* books, vividly describes the destruction of corn and oat crops caused by crows, and the drastic consequences this had for her family. Men like Charles Ingalls relied on the money earned by the crops to pay taxes and buy essential fuel in the winter to keep the family warm. Without a crop he was faced with the option of either using savings, or selling something valuable – in this case a cow – or risk losing his home, or his eldest daughter's opportunity of going to college. With the stakes so high, it is not surprising that enterprising men throughout the ages developed an assortment of tools and devices aimed at preventing and minimizing damage caused by pests.

In Britain the problems caused by vermin or pests were deemed serious enough to require the full-time employment of men to combat them. These men became masters of the trade of pest control and were given titles such as: 'rat catcher', 'mole catcher' or 'warrener', and boys were given the seasonal duty of scaring birds from crops using wooden clappers. In some circumstances pest control was left to field sports enthusiasts who, for example, would gladly assemble at a farm with packs of terriers, intent on driving rats from the hayricks, or conceal themselves in hides amidst crops, equipped with guns so that they could shoot pigeons and crows.

During the 1940s and early 1950s, when the rabbit was considered to be the greatest agricultural pest in Britain, a favourite hobby of many boys was ferreting and they could, during one season, catch

Traditional field sports, such as ferreting, justify their activity by controlling pests that are harmful to agriculture production.

A selection of typical tools for the pest controlling smallholder.

thousands of rabbits. Amidst a torrent of controversy the hunt was, until recent times, commonly relied upon to control the population of foxes living in a particular district.

The widespread employment of chemical poisons, which really took hold in the 1950s, ushered in the era of the modern pest control operative who commonly visits farms and industrial buildings. However, as effective as these lethal potions may be, it has long been recognized that an effective pest control programme depends just as much on circumspect management of the environment, buildings, livestock and animal provender.

Consequently, the daily routine of the farmer and smallholder incorporates vital elements of pest control. Spurred on by this awareness – and the many setbacks to their hopes and plans that pests can inflict – many smallholders have taken a keen interest in becoming their own pest controller, recognizing the advantage of being able to take swift action and select a method which complements their ethical and environmental outlook. For instance, there have always been, and continue to be, people who find the action and after-effects of rodenticides, most notably the secondary poisoning of wildlife, objectionable and would sooner avoid it.

It is also fair to say that a person without a thorough knowledge of the animals classified as pests and their various habits is liable to make what will, in the future, prove to be poor judgements concerning the organization of his smallholding and usage of outbuildings. Consequently, it is the intention of this book to equip the smallholder with the knowledge to take practical steps in order to deter pests and the skills to deal with any pests that do breach his defences. The information it contains is based on my own battle with the pests I have encountered during

two decades running a smallholding and incorporates the traditional arts of ferreting and trapping, which I have been able to master thanks to the tutorage of elderly countrymen and many years of practice.

AIMS OF PEST CONTROL

For centuries gardeners, farmers and gamekeepers in this country have realized the necessity of taking measures to deal with pests and it is a reality that the smallholder of today also has to face. There is no doubt that the average smallholding boasts a treasure trove of delicacies that will attract pests from far and wide and these animals will, without hesitation or sympathy, destroy what many hours of hard work have attempted to achieve. The pest control industry can quote statistics which confirm this point of view; however, stark figures printed on a page fail to capture the disappointment felt by the smallholder when the promising vegetables that he has planted and nourished, are found to have been annihilated overnight by voracious rabbits; the annoyance felt when an egg is found that has been stolen and cracked by a magpie's beak; or the sheer dismay of finding a lamb or hen killed by a fox.

As I have discovered, when it is your crops that are plundered or hen house that is raided, you cannot help taking the onslaught personally and, in some cases, blaming yourself for not taking sufficient precautions initially. In order to avoid such incidents happening, a comprehensive pest control programme will take steps to:

- Protect vulnerable livestock such as poultry, new-born lambs and goat kids from predators.
- Protect vital vegetable, fruit and cereal crops, as well as pasture and woodland from damage.

- Safeguard the health of livestock by preventing the spread of animal-borne diseases and parasites, which are chiefly transmitted by rats and mice.
- Ensure that expensive livestock feeds are not stolen or contaminated by birds or rodents.
- Keep outbuildings in a good state of repair in order to deny pests easy access and harbourage.
- Promptly dispose of rubbish, which attracts pests.
- Comply with health and hygiene recommendations in an environment where home produce is gathered for consumption by the household, or members of the public.

In order to achieve these objectives the resolute pest controller has an assortment of weapons in his armoury to select from. Essentially these will enable him to:

- Eradicate pests when appropriate.
- Pest-proof areas that are at risk.
- Repel pests using scare tactics.

This lamb, born blind, is a clear example of an animal vulnerable to predatory attack.

Vegetable growing is an integral part of smallholding.

ABOVE: Livestock feed is expensive and needs protecting from pests.

SKILLS OF THE PEST CONTROLLER

A great deal of pest control undertaken by the smallholder is nothing more than common sense, however, in order to be consistently successful it would be a great benefit for him to acquire the following:

- A thorough understanding of the wildlife inhabiting the environment in which he lives, to ensure that he is capable of identifying any problems that they are capable of causing and take appropriate preventative action.
- The ability to read tracks, trails and droppings left by animals in order to spot the first signs of a pest's presence and correctly attribute any damage that has been caused. Correct identification of any pest is a prerequisite for selecting the most suitable response.

BELOW: A variety of pests will seek to make their homes in dry, warm outbuildings.

- An understanding of the assortment of different methods of control available to the general public, so that the right one is chosen for the particular problem he is confronted with. This includes knowing the finer details involved in: laying poisons, setting traps, shooting air rifles and putting up electric fences; as well as being fully aware of any dangers they may pose to human health or animals – other than the target species – so that appropriate precautions are taken.
- The skills of a competent stockman so that he is able to fulfil his obligation of care to his animals and identify any of their habits that will act like a magnet for pests.

The smallholder should identify natural features on his land where pests can live, such as this gorse bush, which conceals a rabbit warren.

THE LAW AND PEST CONTROL

In addition to the skills already mentioned, it is of paramount importance for the smallholder to be conversant with the many laws dealing with the subject of pest control. The most relevant of these are:

- The Pests Act of 1954
- The Animal Welfare Act of 2006
- The Wildlife and Countryside Act of 1981
- The Spring Traps Approval Order of 1995
- The Control of Pesticide Regulations of 1986
- The Animals By Product Regulations of 2003

Poultry eggs left uncollected act as magnets to magpies.

Essentially the combined objective of these laws is to ensure that all the animals identified as pests are treated as humanely as possible, and that both non-target species and the environment are afforded adequate protection. In practical terms they aim to achieve this by providing strict guidelines on the following:

Food remains and water bowls attract rodents and birds.

- The particular methods that may be used to deal with pests, for example: poison cannot be used against birds and can only be used on rats and mice without a special licence. Only traps that have been approved by MAFF (now known as DEFRA) may be used and any measures taken to deter protected animals must not disturb their home environment.
- How these various methods are employed, for instance: when spring traps are employed they should be placed in tunnels, to avoid catching anything other than the pest in question; when cage traps are used they must be checked at least once every twenty-four hours.
- How to kill pests: this must be done as quickly as possible, with no unnecessary stress or suffering being inflicted on the pest. For this reason, the practice of drowning animals caught in a trap is strictly prohibited.
- How to dispose of dead animals: this must be done in a safe manner so that the bodies of rats, for example, cannot be eaten by wildlife and cause secondary poisoning which has, in the past, been identified as a cause of death in barn owls.

Safety measures play an important part in pest control. Two examples are the inclusion of blue dye in poison and the insistence on placing spring traps within tunnels.

As well as providing what is, in essence, a code of conduct for the amateur pest controller, the law also offers a clear impetus for action by stating that a householder or landowner must control the pests resident on his property. In the event that he fails to do so, the council will take appropriate action, with the householder/landowner covering the expense. A willingness to comply with this recommendation is not merely a matter of sound judgement, it also leads to sensitive stewardship of the land and environment. To allow any type of pest to establish itself unchecked in any location will not only spell trouble for the smallholder, it will also exert an unnatural pressure on the surrounding flora, fauna and wildlife. The most notable example of this is probably the demise of the red squirrel due to the proliferation of its grey relative.

The recommendations framed by the various laws may, at first sight, give the impression that pest control is all about exterminating nuisance animals. However, this is far from the whole story. Of course, every smallholder will face many situations when the deliberate killing of a pest is the only reasonable course of action; however, he will also encounter just as many other situations when a non-lethal method can be applied with the same measure of success. Some of the strategies that can be employed by the smallholder may come

Small holes may be dug approximately 30cm deep for the disposal of poisoned rats and mice.

as a bit of a surprise to someone new to the subject of pest control. For instance, offering wildlife a bit more from the land, in terms of uncultivated corridors around fields may, in some cases, prevent an animal from becoming a pest in the first place.

BELOW: This immature rabbit (top right of photo), grazing the rough ground of the chicken run, did not need controlling because it posed no threat to the chickens and was not damaging pastureland or crops.

chapter two

The Pests and their Habits

As I immersed myself in the task of pest control I realized that, just as a hunter or fisherman has a knowledge born of experience of the animals that he seeks, I would also have to find out as much as I could about the common pests that I could expect to encounter if I was going to stand any chance of controlling their activities.

I quickly gleaned a great deal of information from an assortment of interesting books with titles such as *Mammals of Britain, Their Tracks, Trails and Signs*, which prompted me to spend time observing the wild animals and birds around me. As a smallholder with an interest in pest control I asked myself the following questions as I watched them:

- Where do they make their homes?
- What do they feed on?
- During what time of day or night are they most active?
- Can they climb, squeeze through small gaps or chew holes in wood?
- What signs do they leave on the ground indicative of their presence?

The answers to these questions would, in turn, help me to take informed and decisive action to deal with any pests. They would also provide the basis for the information contained in this chapter, along with an analysis of whether the harm that animals classified as pests cause is, in certain situations, outweighed by any good they do, in terms of predating other pests and eating insects harmful to crops.

In Britain there are a small number of pests capable of killing poultry and ducks, others that damage immature woodland and those that eat crops. However, we shall start our study with an impudent, disease-carrying thief, which is unquestionably the most despised and dreaded pest of all – the rat.

THE RAT

Ever since the brown rat, also known as the Norwegian rat, arrived in Britain around 1760, it has had the capacity to turn robust men and indomitable women into quivering wrecks, in spite of the fact that it is no more than 25cm long, including the tail, and weighs 200g, which is roughly 300 times less than the average adult. Is the panic they engender therefore totally irrational, or do we have just cause for being especially wary of the rat?

Following its introduction the brown rat quickly spread throughout the British Isles and, in the process, displaced the plague-carrying black rat, which had brought so

Areas that are left to grow wild will provide cover for pests, however, some will also find their food in such places instead of eating crops.

much sorrow to families across the land, especially during the seventeenth century. The supplanting of the black rat by the brown was aided by improvements in rubbish disposal and sanitation, and a shift from building in wood to brick and stone.

It did not take long, however, for the brown rat to make a nuisance of itself in both the town and the countryside. Those whose job it was to deal with the burgeoning population of brown rats succumbed to a mystery illness, which became known as 'rat catcher's yellows', owing to the colour of the sufferers, who rarely survived more than a week from the time they contracted the disease. The 'yellows', or Weil's disease to give it its correct medical name, remains with us today, with the brown rat being the principal carrier of the disease, although the number of fatalities

in recent years is minuscule in comparison to the numbers who succumbed during the nineteenth century, when people were far less cautious about handling rats. While there are an assortment of alarming tales relating experiences of being bitten by ferocious rats it is, above all, the disease-carrying characteristic that threatens the health of humans and their livestock, which has earned the brown rat the unabated and warranted antipathy of man.

Consequently, the chief reason for controlling rats is to prevent the spread of disease, which is transmitted in their urine and excreta, and thus safeguard our own health and that of the valuable animals we rely upon to provide us with food. As a result of the study of epidemiology, medical researchers have highlighted groups of people who are more at risk from Weil's disease than the general public. The list includes sewage workers, which most of us would expect but a startling fact is that more farmers than sewage workers have contracted the disease in recent years. This highlights how careful the smallholder has to be, since the environment in which he lives and tends his stock is markedly similar to that of the farmer.

Whether you regard it as an opportunistic feeder or a thief, the rat will, given the slightest chance, plunder the grain store and raid the poultry shed in order to satisfy its appetite. Although there are accounts, verified with some remarkable photographs, of industrious rats stealing eggs from chicken sheds, they are more likely to concentrate their energies on the many grain derivatives that are fed to livestock. In the process of eating, rats will contaminate the grain with their hair, faeces and urine and so render it unsafe for livestock consumption. It is estimated that in a year one rat will produce as much as 6l of urine and 15,000 droppings and shed approximately 300,000 hairs; it therefore

The typical gnawing damage of a rodent attempting to gain access to a barn.

has the capacity to ruin many costly bags of stored grain if left unchecked. The loss of 20 per cent of the world's stored grain to rats, perfectly illustrates this point.

To get at what they want determined rats will, with their incredibly sharp and powerful teeth, gnaw their way through wood and have been known to penetrate 5cm piping to get at water. Their capacity to gnaw at anything that gets in their

way, combined with their ability to scale walls and burrow under floors, means that there are few places they are not capable of gaining access to and they have rightly been described as ruthless destroyers of property. Investigations have revealed that fire damage and burst water pipes in many farm buildings is attributable to resident rats chewing through electric cables and plastic pipes.

Unfortunately, there is no getting away from rats: they are as common in the town as they are in the countryside and as much at home on a farm as in an industrial warehouse, which is why they are considered one of the most adaptable mammals in the world. On the farm or smallholding rats tend to live in burrows along hedgerows and ditches, underneath sheds and in hay ricks and farm buildings. However, they have no rule book to abide by when establishing a home for themselves and, in typical feats of initiative, will utilize whatever materials are available. I have encountered rats living in log piles, under the tarpaulin of a covered muck heap, beneath corrugated metal sheets that were left lying on the ground and in cavities dug through the lime render between the rocks of a hard granite wall. They do possess a keenness for making their nests at ground level, with a supply of water nearby which they cannot do without. This water source may be a stream, ditch, drain, pond, leaking pipe or animal drinker and, in their desire to drink, many juvenile rats have been found drowned in buckets of water in stables and goat houses.

Essentially rats search for somewhere to nest where they will remain warm, dry and go unnoticed. They choose a site where

Old stone walls near poultry and fowl make ideal homes for rats.

A disused barn with thick straw left on the ground will provide an ideal home for rats.

they will not have to travel far to secure their daily requirement of food and water, and the less open ground they have to cross in the process the better. Typically they do not like wandering more than 50m from their nests and will follow established paths, usually along walls or hedges, to and from their destination. Peak times of activity are at dusk and during the night, which is why some old countrymen used to routinely take their dogs outdoors just as it was getting dark and conduct what they referred to as a 'rat patrol'. In this manner the well known writer and countryman, Phil Drabble, with the assistance of his two dogs, accounted for 200 rats in one year. The sight of rats during daylight hours is usually indicative of a substantial infestation or, in the case of a single rat, a sick animal.

Within the nest rats multiply speedily, with a pair of rats being capable of producing eighty offspring in just one year. As rats can breed when they are ten weeks old and have on average six litters a year, it is easy to see how just two rats could lay the foundation for a colony of many thousands and, being naturally gregarious, they are quite content to live communally. The rapidity with which rats can increase in number is a problem because there are always more to fill the space left by those that are trapped, poisoned or shot and current estimates are that there are a minimum of eighty million rats in Britain.

Fortunately for the pest controller, rats leave an assortment of signs that are easy to identify, which prove their presence on a property. In addition to the damage caused by gnawing alluded to earlier these signs include:

- Droppings – these are large and cylindrical in shape, measuring 17mm by 6mm. An assortment of different-sized droppings is suggestive of a breeding colony.
- Smears – this refers to greasy marks or stains left on solid objects, owing to the rats' preference for moving with their bodies in direct contact with the objects.
- Tracks – footprints will register in mud, dust and snow, with feet pointing outwards and a typical stride of 9–10cm.
- Runs – these are narrow, well trodden paths, approximately 10–15cm wide, that are clearly visible in any vegetation around or near outbuildings.

The rat is a very cautious animal by nature and is sensitive to any changes that occur in the environment it has grown accustomed to; this fact must be borne in mind when laying poisons or setting traps. A rat's reaction whenever it comes face to face with humans is always to flee, which it tends to do at considerable speed. It was while I was watching some rats escaping from a barn that I realized what small gaps they

This shows the average size and typical colour and shape of the brown rat.

can squeeze through to effect their getaway – some of the holes that they negotiated quite effortlessly were no more than 35mm in diameter. I could not help thinking that the rats had a prearranged escape plan as they fled, without any apparent hesitation or thought concerning which was the best way to go. In this case I was expecting them to try and make a dash for the wide barn door but, instead, they clawed their way up a 2m granite wall and departed through the semi-circular spaces created by the union of the corrugated metal roof with the wall. While it was frustrating to watch the rats escape, it did help me to realize just how easy it can be for a determined rat to gain access to an outbuilding.

Although rats will flee when discovered by humans, they can sometimes be very sly and will tolerate people virtually walking over them when they are confident in their ability to remain hidden. I remember on one occasion my Jack Russell terrier, after much digging and grumbling, emerging from a goat pen that had been lined with a thick bed of straw, with a large doe rat in his mouth. Despite a constant traffic of people going in and out of the pen, the rat had not felt the need to bolt, simply because the covering of straw kept it out of sight. There is no doubt how alarmed people feel when they find out that they have been happily undertaking their daily tasks with a rat sometimes no more than a couple of feet away from them; it is equally true that having rats in or near animal housing does rob some people of their enthusiasm for, and enjoyment of, tending their stock.

In many respects rats appear to be invincible. They can flourish in the most squalid conditions, on a diet so putrefied that the ptomaine levels would kill a vulture, while efforts to reduce their numbers are constantly frustrated by their prolific reproductive rate. Such characteristics would not be so threatening if the rats were stupid, clumsy and carefree, instead of intelligent, agile and cautious.

With rats being such formidable antagonists, innovative humans have developed a variety of techniques that can be utilized by the smallholder to eradicate any that appear on his land or in his buildings. Foremost among them are poisoning with a difenacoum-based rodenticide and trapping with a spring trap, such as the Fenn Mark VI. Other methods include the employment of a live trap, the use of dogs and ferrets and shooting with an air weapon.

The smallholder should use every means at his disposal to deal with rats as quickly as possible. As field sports enthusiast and journalist Jack Ivester Lloyd stated in an article he wrote in 1969: 'Whether described as vermin or pest, everyone is out to destroy the rat by any means that are at hand.'

THE HOUSE MOUSE

In many ways house mice are similar to rats; certainly in appearance they look like tiny versions of brown rats and it has been known for people to confuse them with immature rats. However, the house mouse has much larger ears in relation to its head than the brown rat. In colour it is greyish brown above, merging into greyish buff below.

Like rats, mice can be very destructive and are capable of transmitting diseases, such as salmonella, which can cause food poisoning. A preference for living inside, combined with their breeding habits, means that mice are able to rapidly colonize the smallholder's outbuilding, where electric cables and insulation will be vulnerable to their incessant gnawing. Any type of livestock feed or stored grain attracts the

A house mouse.

attention of their acute noses and they have a tendency to chew through the bottom corners of 25kg sacks to get at the cereal-based contents they contain. While the volume they consume may not be that considerable, the fact that they dribble urine constantly and are hosts of harmful bacteria, renders any food they trample over unfit for use.

Denying mice access to buildings can prove very difficult because of their minuscule size and ability to flatten their bodies, so that they can squeeze through gaps as small as 6mm. In buildings constructed of wood, or with wooden floors, they will use their teeth like little saws to widen cracks into small holes that they can then push their bodies through.

Once inside a building, mice are masters at concealing their nests in straw, hay or any discarded soft material and can, therefore, reside inside for some time before they actually get noticed. Being so small and light they leave no observable footprints or trail, but they do give themselves away by depositing copious amounts of black droppings, which are about 3mm long, on floors and surfaces, such as feed benches. If there is any livestock feed present they tend to discard the outer husks of the grain in a random manner and may leave tiny teeth marks in the larger flakes, such as peas and maize. Although grain and grain products, such as bread, are the favoured food of mice they can survive on such odd items as plaster, soap and wood. They will also eat vegetables and there are cases of mice inhabiting polytunnels, which provide them with both warmth and a constant supply of food. Unlike the rat, the mouse does not need to be near water because it extracts sufficient fluid for its survival from the food it digests.

For such small animals, mice can make a lot of noise when they are on the move, but this is usually only ever heard by people

The appearance of droppings, as seen in this live trap, is an obvious sign of the presence of mice.

Using his powers of scent and hearing, this terrier can detect and catch mice hiding in animal bedding.

when the mice are residing within the four walls of a house. They can also be quite vocal and emit a high-pitched squeak. While it is unlikely that a person is going to be able to discern these sounds inside a barn, a dog often will, if it is allowed the freedom to root about. My Jack Russell terrier is a very accomplished mouser and daily makes an inspection of the goat barn. If he comes to a halt, tilts his head in a strangely robotic manner and begins to tremble from nose to tail, I know that he is listening to mice. The house mouse also has a distinctive, unpleasant, musty smell, which can also be detected by a keen dog.

Like rats, mice are most active during the night, when there is less chance of them being disturbed by the presence of people. Although they are very easily scared and

will take fright at the slightest noise, house mice are also great adventurers and seem compelled to examine any new item that is placed in their environment. This bizarre mix of excessive timidity and curiosity does mean that they are much easier to trap than rats.

In habitats that are peaceful, mice may undertake a small amount of daytime activity, so long as they do not have to move over any areas of open ground. They prefer staying close to walls and moving through and under obstacles such as pallets, sacks and stored wood. On those rare occasions when mice are spotted travelling during the day, it has been known for people to catch them by hand and my late grandfather had a particular talent for this.

Just as in the case of the brown rat, the control of mice requires an ongoing and determined effort by the smallholder and daily inspections should be carried out, looking for the signs indicative of their presence. The most commonly used methods for dealing with mice are poison, containing a combination of calciferol and difenacoum, traditional mouse traps, known as break-back traps, live traps and sonic repellers.

THE FIELD MOUSE

As well as the house mouse, I encounter a lot of field mice mounting raids on my storage sheds and visiting my barns during the autumn and winter months. Lionel E. Adams conducted a lengthy study of the field mouse during the early part of the twentieth century and published his findings in a 1914 edition of the *Wild Life Journal*. According to him field mice can be found in: woods, hedges, corn fields and dry stone walls. In fact they have been spotted nearly anywhere: from the seashore, to the tops of the hills; they have even been found residing in deep, disused mines and it has also been said that every decent sized garden will have some field mice living in it.

The field mouse is much more striking than the house mouse, due to its different coloured coat. It is brown above, which contrasts distinctly with a white neck and underbelly. It also boasts long hind feet, sometimes measuring as much as 20mm and is, by mice standards, quite large, generally with a body size of approximately 9cm in length.

Like the house mouse, the field mouse is most active during the hours of darkness and is rarely spotted during the day. Being an expert climber and able to squeeze through the tiniest of gaps, there are few structures that will keep out determined field mice

and many cellars used as vegetable stores have been breached by them. They will happily gnaw on any type of root vegetable and, in doing so, will render what has been harvested and carefully stored to see the smallholder through the winter, unfit for consumption. There are few more frustrating experiences than opening the door of a root cellar or shed, only to find provisions that were being counted upon vandalised by mice. However, the mischief they inflict on the vegetable grower is not restricted to autumn and winter. During the spring they have been known to devastate gardens and are unrelenting thieves of newly sown beans and peas. This has resulted in the field mouse being called the 'bean mouse', or 'beaner' in the counties of Surrey, Sussex and Kent. They can also cause substantial damage to sprouting wheat and newly planted crops.

As winter approaches, they begin to lay up stores in the burrows where they generally live. The burrow is identified by a small heap of ejected earth 7–9cm high and 30cm in diameter, which looks very much like a small mole hill and is often mistaken for one. These ground nests are usually situated in hedgerows or among farm crops, however, there are also accounts of field mice being found nesting

Mice are fast moving and can jump remarkable distances for their size.

The field mouse has large ears and a white underbelly.

in rooks' nests in tall trees. Acorns and hazelnuts form the commonest provisions and a store can sometimes be found in the corner of a barn or outhouse.

They will wander along the branches of hedges in search of hips and haws and will sometimes retire to an old bird's nest to eat what they have gathered, although they are much more likely to feed on the ground and the debris of their meals under hawthorn bushes is a common sight. The only parts of the hips and haws that they eat are the kernels of the seed and they gather this fruit by biting it off within 6mm of the stalk. Field mice do occasionally suck the yolk from the eggs of small birds and will happily eat the body of a dead comrade without hesitation; the skin of a mouse left in a ragged heap is a sure indicator that this has taken place.

The field mouse is small, quick moving, evasive and a capable climber. It can claw its way through tiny gaps, leap considerable distances from a starting position, and jump from heights well in excess of 2m and land on concrete floors without causing itself any injury. Clearly these attributes combined make the field mouse one of, if not *the* most difficult animal to exclude

from outbuildings that the smallholder will encounter.

However, an awareness of the weather's impact on the creature's food reserves will enable the smallholder to anticipate its visitation and make adequate preparations. In my own case, as a resident of the chilly north-east of Scotland, I can expect field mice from the month of November onwards to make serious and continuous efforts to enter my barns in search of any cereals that they can find left in feed buckets, or spilt on the floor. Consequently, in combination with making the buildings as impregnable as possible, I endeavour to keep them well swept and tidy and deploy both multi-catch live traps and break-back traps. Additional strategies for dealing with field mice include preserving the wildlife that prey on them such as: kestrels, barn owls, tawny owls, stoats and weasels, as well as keeping a resident cat and the use of sonic repellers.

THE GREY SQUIRREL

In Britain the grey squirrel is not regarded with the same affection as it is in its native North American homeland. Principally this is because its presence in this country is viewed as the largest contributing factor to the demise of our quaint, indigenous red squirrel. Consequently, the grey is nearly as unpopular as the brown rat and there are some who advocate its complete eradication from the British countryside, in order to promote the red squirrel. Others feel that this might be a step too far and view the extermination of grey squirrels from areas where they are already established as impractical. They suggest that efforts should be concentrated on keeping the localities where red squirrels are resident free from greys. It is forgotten that, in the past, man played a significant part in reducing the numbers of red squirrels, because of the damage they were causing to trees. A clear example is the Highland Squirrel Club, which, between 1900 and 1946, killed over 100,000 red squirrels.

Primarily these are issues for conservationists to grapple with and are unlikely to influence the smallholder who has grey squirrels living on his land, unless he happens to be living in one of the red squirrel sensitive zones. What does directly concern the smallholder however, is whether grey squirrels pose a realistic threat to those things that he is endeavouring to grow and rear. Unfortunately for the grey squirrel it has, in the past, been found guilty of a long list of offences. Included amongst these are: damage to trees, theft of ripening fruit, consumption of arable crops, killing of game and poultry chicks, and feasting upon feed intended for livestock. However, recent studies have revealed that substantial damage is a direct result of a high density of squirrels in one location and a reduction in their numbers can often prove to be an effective remedy.

The grey squirrel was brought to the British Isles during the latter part of the nineteenth century by various aristocratic families, who released them in the substantial grounds and parks surrounding their stately homes. Since that time they have spread to most parts of England, Wales and southern and central Scotland. They make their homes wherever trees are to be found; whether it is extensive mixed woodland or isolated stumps of standards and, if seed-bearing hardwoods are found close to coniferous plantations, they too will be colonized.

The squirrel lives in a nest known as a drey, which is made of an assortment of twigs and bark, lined with moss, dry leaves, grass and occasionally animal fur. These are located in the large fork of a tree and look like large, round bird's nests, sometimes as big as a football. Occasionally squirrels make their dreys inside the trunks of hollow trees.

The grey squirrel is slightly larger than the red, measuring 45–60cm long and typically weighing 500–650g. As the name suggests, this squirrel is essentially grey in appearance, however, closer inspection reveals hairs of an assortment of colours. The underfur is the shade of lead and the long guard hairs are tan near the base, black in the centre and tipped with white. On the top of the head, back, legs and saddle, the grey is tinged with brownish yellow and, in

Live traps are considered one of the best ways to catch grey squirrels.
STV INTERNATIONAL

some cases, this has been so distinctive that the squirrel has been mistaken for one of its red relatives. The cheeks, muzzle, ear and underparts of the paw on most specimens are a clear tan. The long tail hairs, like those of the body, end in white and give the tail a silvery appearance.

The grey squirrel is often referred to as a 'tree rat' and it does, in fact, belong to the rodent family and possesses the distinctive, razor-edged, chisel-like teeth, capable of gnawing through hardwood and nuts. When doing so, it has the ability to suck in its cheeks to prevent sawdust going down its throat. They usually spend more time aloft than on the ground, with long toes and curved claws helping them cling to branches. Forays onto the ground will be taken when food is scarce.

Squirrels have keen eyesight that alerts them to danger and, when frightened, the grey will quickly take to the nearest tree and can run along the branches at a swift 30kph. It has also cultivated the skill of always keeping the tree trunk between itself and its enemies. If need be the grey squirrel will, without hesitation, leap from the highest branches of a tree; on such occasions its large, bushy tail serves as both a rudder and a parachute. Should it miss a branch – which it rarely does – and come hurtling to the ground, it does not seem to matter for the grey squirrel dashes to the nearest tree without a pause. The ability to freeze and lie motionless along a branch is the squirrel's second line of defence and, in such a position, is virtually invisible even to the keenest of observers.

Although squirrels are diurnal, they are most active just after daylight when the first rays of the morning sun are glinting through the tree tops. Displaying a great deal of common sense, the grey is inactive on wet stormy days, preferring instead to stay within the comfort of the drey. It is a creature of catholic taste and the

typical diet includes: soft fruit, fungi, grain, catkins, insects and nuts. It will usually have a favourite place to feed, such as a tree stump or branch and the accumulation of food remnants will enable the smallholder to identify its location. During the autumn the grey squirrel will eat as much as it can and then begin burying food in shallow troughs as stores for winter, relying on its keen sense of smell to rediscover these stores when they are needed.

Bark stripping is regarded as the chief crime committed by the grey squirrel, with the healthiest trees, usually aged between ten and forty years old, being singled out for attack as the squirrels attempt to get at the inner sap. Sycamore, oak, beech, sweet chestnut, pine, larch and Norway spruce are most susceptible to damage, although most broadleaves are vulnerable. However, this only occurs for four months of the year, from the end of April to the end of July, and it has been calculated that only 3 per cent of those trees that are damaged will actually decay and die. This knowledge enables the smallholder to take suitable measures to protect his trees and recently a spray has been introduced, utilizing capsicum as its main ingredient, which, when applied

Although essentially grey in colour, close inspection reveals hairs of an assortment of colours.

Good quality pasture is essential for livestock, such as this heavy horse, to thrive.

regularly deters the squirrel from showing an interest in the treated tree. The most effective, tried and tested way to control grey squirrel damage to woodland is to employ live capture traps and spring traps placed in tunnels.

Shooting has always been a popular method of dealing with squirrels and, in their native homeland, the early settlers would shoot vast numbers of the species owing to its popularity as a food item. A special gun was designed for this purpose that became known as the 'Kentucky Squirrel Rifle'. For those hunting the squirrel in Britain today, the air rifle will prove equally suitable for the task. Of course, for those selecting this method, the correct identification of quarry is paramount; for those in any doubt the description of coat colour included in this section should serve as an accurate guide.

There is no doubt that the grey squirrel can be a fascinating animal to watch as it performs acrobatic feats worthy of the very best circuses. However, it can also prove to be an absolute menace to fruit and vegetable growers and those rearing game or poultry chicks. Squirrels quickly become familiar with humans and will, after a short period of time, be emboldened to treat the smallholding as if it is their own. The only option available to those who do not wish to use a fatal method of control, is to utilize some form of crop protection and secure runs for rearing chicks, however these can

be costly because of the gauge of wire required.

THE MOLE

Unlike rats and mice, the mole is a creature that has been written about, rather confusingly, as a pest to man in some situations and as a helper in others. The name mole is a shortened version of the old English name for the animal, 'moldwarp', which means a thrower up of the earth and it is this excavation of soil that can produce problems for farmers and gardeners alike. No landowner wishes to see his valuable pasture or hay meadows littered with mole hills, which lead to soil fouling of silage and, when large stones are thrown up, damage to mowers. Additionally, the mole is known to cause root damage to plants, grass and crops and may, unwittingly, transport diseased organisms from one affected plant to another. The quality of the pasture may also be degraded, as the fresh heaps of soil make ideal seed beds for undesirable, vigorous growing plants which are not heavily grazed, such as bent grasses, buttercups and nettles.

Defenders of the mole make the counter-claim that the little damage done by the creature is as nothing compared with the great good that it does. They suggest that, wherever you see a chain of mole hills running across a field, you can rest assured that the mole is busy killing some of the farmer's enemies, such as wireworms and leather jackets. In contradiction to the previous statement regarding the quality of the pasture, some farmers have apparently acknowledged that sheep and cattle thrive best in mole-infested fields. They believe that the earth thrown up on the hillocks and exposed to the air becomes so fertile that the best grass grows there; a dressing of this earth has even been used in the past to make good pastures at small cost.

All of this presents the smallholder with a dilemma: should he initiate some form of mole control or leave the industrious little creature to work away on his behalf? Clearly, when the damage the moles are causing far outweighs any good they are capable of doing, then something needs to be done. Obvious examples are fields such as the one I observed, where sheep were finding it increasingly difficult to graze because the moles were rapidly turning it into a field

A typical pattern of mole hills.

that contained more soil than grass. Equally undesirable is a mole tunnelling into the vegetable plot where it disturbs, albeit unintentionally, carefully cultivated seed drills. Therefore the incentive for action is based upon the intensity of mole activity and the location where such activity is taking place.

As principally a subterranean dweller, the mole is rarely seen, although the products of its labour are all too apparent. Armed with immense spade-like hands, the mole is a prolific tunneller. The soil, which they displace during the course of their excavating, must go somewhere and is ejected upwards, through sloping and vertical shafts and presents two distinctive patterns, which indicate the depth at which the mole is digging. Above ground, small piles of earth in a line indicate deep tunnelling, while continuous lines of earth at the surface represent shallow tunnels at root level. The depth of the tunnel itself is influenced by the location of worms and the weather. In dry conditions the mole tends to have to dig deeper to catch worms which, along with insects, larvae, millipedes and slugs, make up its diet.

The tunnels are, in effect, traps that the mole has skilfully constructed to catch its prey, most commonly worms as they move through the soil, and which the mole detects with its finely attuned nose. A rudimentary survey of the anatomy of the mole shows that its whole body has been designed for burrowing. It is cylindrical in shape, the limbs are short, thick and powerful, the immense shovel-like hands face outwards to facilitate digging and it has a pointed muzzle, which it can thrust through the earth like a battering ram.

Although the mole tends to sleep every four hours, it is very industrious when awake and is reputed to be able to dig 2m in ten minutes. When it is not digging the mole diligently patrols the

The mole has tiny eyes, which are barely perceptible.

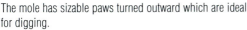

The mole has sizable paws turned outward which are ideal for digging.

tunnels, in order to acquire enough food to satisfy its voracious appetite. A mole will consume the equivalent of its body weight, 60–120g, each day. With the exception of the breeding season, the mole is a solitary figure that is so aggressive towards other moles that, should their territories overlap and paths cross, they will engage in such fierce combat that one of them will be killed. The typical male range is one eighth of an acre and the female one twelfth. This knowledge enables the smallholder to estimate, with a reasonable degree of accuracy, the number of moles resident on his land at any given time.

Moles are found throughout Britain and can survive in all soil types, although sand and chalk are least favoured. They particularly like pasture, arable farmland, open heath and woodland. At such sites, a mole will construct a home, known as a fortress or palace, which is most commonly situated beneath unbroken soil, but can also appear as a large heap or mole hill. These can extend to 2.4m in diameter and

be as much as 60cm high and typically contain a maze of passages that serve as entrance, exit and escape routes. It will contain a central chamber, filled with a round mass of dried grass and leaves. This is the mole's nest in which, in early spring and late summer, the young are born naked, blind and helpless.

In the past an assortment of homemade remedies were tried in an attempt to deal with moles, ranging from resting a milk bottle on top of a mole hill, to piercing one of the tunnels with a spade. Trapping is the traditional method for controlling moles and, up until the commencement of the Second World War, the fur trade used the skins to make waistcoats and would pay nine pence for each one. Amidst concerns that the mole could contribute to a reduction in home food production, and with many of the skilled trappers serving in the armed forces during the war, strychnine was employed and worms containing the poison would be placed in the tunnels frequented by the mole.

The muzzle is suitably shaped for thrusting through the earth.

Studies have shown that the practice of trapping with the traditional spring traps remains the most effective means of control. Two such traps are available: the pincer or scissors trap and the duffus or half-barrel trap, with the names indicating the shape or pattern of the trap. Other control measures include: repellents, such as ultrasonic devices and the placing of strong smelling substances within the tunnels, such as mole smokes, which generate castor oil fumes that drive the mole away, but are only effective for a limited duration. In order to be able to utilize any of these methods, a practical knowledge of the construction of the mole's labyrinth of tunnels is required.

THE RABBIT

The rabbit, like the mole, is considered a pest owing to the damage it does to pasture and crops; however, unlike the mole this is not due to the excavation of the soil, but the consumption of crops. Prior to the introduction of myxomatosis in 1953, the rabbit had the singular honour of being ranked as the most troublesome pest to British agriculture and caused millions of pounds' worth of damage each year. The fact that the meat of the wild rabbit played a significant part in the national diet and the skins were utilized by the fur trade, did not compensate sufficiently for the amount of damage they were deemed to cause to the production of human food. Myxomatosis appeared to be an easy way to solve the problem and control the numbers of rabbits, however, it came with a number of drawbacks. There was no way to control it once it was unleashed and it resulted in the complete waste of a natural resource; 99 per cent of the rabbit population was wiped out in a manner which public opinion swiftly turned against. Onlookers were appalled as they beheld rabbits with swollen, pustulated eyes and emaciated bodies, dying a slow death.

Although myxomatosis devastated rabbits throughout all of Britain's countryside, this tenacious animal has managed to re-establish itself in all parts of the country and is once again flourishing and getting up to its old, familiar tricks. The chief offences are the consumption of arable crops, grazing of pasture and debarking of young growing trees, all of which are likely to enrage the smallholder, just as much as the farmer. Combined with the speed with which the rabbit can increase its numbers and colonize an area, there is no doubt that rabbit numbers need to be controlled and there is now a consensus of opinion that this should be done in a way that is both humane and also enables the meat and skin of the animal to be used.

Belonging to the family Leporida, the rabbit possesses certain distinctive features, which are: long ears, long hind limbs and eyes that are placed at the side of the

Although the rabbit may at times be a pest, it can also be a welcome source of food.

of the head. The ears have large flaps, which can be turned to catch the slightest sound, and the eyes can scan a wide arc to detect any predators. The back legs are approximately three times the length of the front ones and enable the rabbit to catapult itself explosively forward and sprint at great speed. The hind legs are also a drawback for the rabbit however, because they leave an unmistakeable trail in soft ground. Additional indicators of its presence in the countryside include: narrow 8cm, well-trodden pathways; indiscriminate diggings or shallow, bowl-shaped scrapings in the ground; rabbit droppings, which are the size of a sultana and usually left in clusters in shallow depressions in the earth or on a rock; fur caught on fences and hedges; warrens and, of course, crop damage. The nature of this crop damage may be tender young vegetable plants eaten back to their stems, or root crops exposed and lumps bitten out of them.

Although the rabbit is most active during the hours of darkness, it will venture out during the day in quiet locations where humans and predators are either absent, or at a safe distance. Even so, the crafty rabbit will usually stay within bolting distance of its underground hideaway that, for such a quick running animal can be as much as 100m. At

Tree damage caused by rabbits during the winter, when snow was covering the ground.

the first sign of danger the rabbit will either dash as fast as it can to the warren or crouch down, pressing its body firmly into the ground and remain there motionless, in the hope that its grey-brown coat will enable it to merge into the surrounding landscape and so go undetected.

The rabbit's typical home is known as a warren and consists of an interconnected system of tunnels, terminating in a procession of holes at ground level. The extent of an individual warren will depend upon the number of rabbits living together. Warrens are most often found at the base of hedges, or on the slopes of banks or ditches, which are usually near to a good feeding ground. Sometimes rabbits will utilize the shelter and protection afforded by sheds, log piles or rocks, particularly as a temporary refuge during the day.

Like the brown rat, one of the reasons why rabbits must be controlled is because of

their prolific rate of multiplication. Rabbits give birth during the warmer months of the year, however, mild autumns and winters can result in extended breeding seasons. A litter consists of between six and fourteen babies and these are not born in the warren, but in a specially constructed, one-hole tunnel known as a stop, which the mother, who only attends her offspring for brief periods each day, blocks with soil after each visit.

When in search of food the rabbit can show determination and enterprise and it can prove to be a very difficult animal to keep out. As a capable digger, it can quickly find its way under fences and is able to squeeze through gaps as small as 12cm in diameter. It can also easily chew its way through standard, nylon garden netting that is being used to protect vegetables. With regard to rabbit damage to pasture, this simply refers to the consumption of grass by the rabbits. Although the smallholder may not have the density of livestock that a farmer does, he has a much smaller area of land for his grazing animals to feed on. With just five rabbits eating the equivalent of one sheep, it is evident that an unchecked colony of rabbits will place a considerable strain on the pasture and may lead to a situation where supplementary feeds are required to maintain the grazing livestock in the best condition. This will, in turn, lead to an additional expenditure that can be easily avoided.

In Britain rabbits have been viewed, at times, as the most dangerous animals to forestry. The time when rabbits are most likely to attack young trees is during frosty weather, especially when the ground is covered with snow. They do prefer soft-barked types of trees but, as all kinds of

When startled a rabbit will either bolt or crouch down and flatten its ears in the hope that it will go undetected.

Although rabbits are most commonly grey in colour, there are also some that are black.

trees have soft bark while young, none are safe where rabbits abound. The worst damage is done during severe winters and it has been known for their stripping of bark to cause the death of big, old park trees. Attempts were made to deter rabbits, which included smearing trees with evil smelling substances, but this had very mixed results. Much more effective was the use of close meshed wire fencing and it became common practice to protect a plantation for a period of seven years.

The smallholder has numerous methods that he can either select from, or use in conjunction, to control rabbits effectively. Unlike the case of rodents, the aim of rabbit control is not the complete removal of the species from the smallholding, but the careful management of their numbers, which, in turn, restricts the amount of damage that they can cause. By routinely walking around his fields when it is dark and sweeping torchlight in an arc over the ground, the smallholder will be able to spot rabbits, estimate their strength and consequently assess the likely extent of any damage and take appropriate precautions. A combination of some form

of crop protection, such as electric fencing or polytunnels, and culling with ferrets or an air rifle, is an ideal strategy for the smallholder. Other tools that can be used to deal with rabbits include: chemical and sonic repellents, live capture traps and the conservation of natural predators such as foxes and stoats.

THE BROWN HARE

The brown hare is, in many respects, a larger and heavier version of a rabbit. It belongs to the same family, Leporidae, and has the same distinctive anatomical peculiarities, although hares are somewhat bigger. It has a similar gait to the rabbit and moves by a series of leaps. Hares and rabbits cannot walk as such and even the slowest movements are in the form of leaps and hops, which leave very distinctive tracks. There are, however, some subtle differences in the appearance and habits of brown hares compared to rabbits. The hare has black tips to its ears and a much browner coat, which moults twice a year to the rabbit's once.

A flattened area in long grass is a sign of a hare.

Behaviourally hares are solitary animals; they do not burrow and live above, rather than below ground, in a resting place known as a form. The form is usually a concealed spot, flattened out in grass or thick herbage, which the hare nestles into to gain shelter from the weather and secure concealment from predators. Both its colouring and stillness when in the form enable it to blend seamlessly into the surrounding landscape. It does this to such good effect that many walkers have confirmed that they have only became aware of the hare's presence by nearly stepping on it. The hare will usually have a number of forms to choose from within its territory and even the young, known as leverets, are reared in forms. However, unlike rabbits, leverets are born with a full body of fur and their eyes and ears open.

Whereas the rabbit likes the shelter of bushes, the hare is essentially an animal of the open spaces, favouring big arable fields and rolling downland. It can speed lightly across the turf on the long legs that propel it with ease, at speeds in excess of those achieved by both greyhounds and horses. Although hares are essentially solitary animals, they often choose to feed communally during the hours of darkness, obviously deriving a greater sense of security from being in a group. The signs left by hares are similar to those left by rabbits and include: damage to growing crops; debarking of young trees; narrow well worn pathways; slightly flattened droppings of 1.5cm in diameter; hair left in forms during spring and autumn moults and tracks left in soft ground. For food, hares require short growing crops: grass, herbs, post-harvest stubble and weeds and will not trouble fields containing grown cereal crops.

The brown hare has never rivalled the rabbit as a leading pest of British agriculture and has generally been treated much more sympathetically than rabbits by farmers. This is probably because the damage caused is far less noticeable, as hares tend to move through fields leaving little patches of grazed areas. Another reason is that hares do not multiply as quickly as rabbits, in fact they are relatively scarce in many parts of Britain, largely due to their inability to adapt to modern agricultural practices, which result in food scarcity for the animal at vital times of the year. Consequently, the hare is not often found in sufficient numbers to be a troublesome pest to the smallholder; this fact is attested to by professional pest controllers, such as George Hogg who, in the course of writing his book *Practical Pest Control* states that he had only killed one hare in many years and even then it was only because it was attacking a young fir plantation.

Unlike rodents that are unequivocally deemed a pest whenever they appear,

Hares favour large open fields.

the brown hare is only occasionally a pest and does not need to be exiled from the smallholding. On the contrary, the smallholder, who generally has a far less intensive land management regime than the farmer, is ideally suited to conserve the hare by providing grass borders around, and corridors between fields, leaving stubble fields unploughed until the succeeding crop is due to be sown. All of this contributes to the provision of a much needed food source and prevents the hare having to turn its attention to crops or trees. Tree guards, electric fencing and wire netting may also be effectively employed to protect young saplings and crops from hares.

DEER

Deer are regal-looking creatures and I recall, when three appeared in a field near my home, being so captivated by the sight of them that I gave absolutely no thought to any damage they could cause. As enchanting as they are, it is a well documented fact that deer are in possession of dietary motivated habits which result in noticeable damage, primarily to woodland and, to a lesser extent, vegetable and cereal crops, with damage proving most serious in those parts of the country where deer have not been well managed.

The damage that deer cause to trees is identical to that inflicted by the domestic goat if given an opportunity, and many smallholders will be familiar with the tell-tale signs. They are able to nibble into the bark and tear it off in strips, completely debarking a tree in a remarkably short space of time. Younger trees are preferred and usually will not exceed 7.5cm diameter. Tree damage can also result from bucks rubbing their horns vigorously against the pliable trunk, sometimes bending and splitting it, although more commonly cutting into it. The buck does this to mark his territory, or when he wants to remove the skin, referred to as velvet, from his antlers when they are fully grown: a process known as fraying. Although vegetable and cereal crops are more rarely selected by the deer, when they are inclined they have the capacity to tear the green tops off root crops such as swedes and carrots and gobble up the leaves of brassicas, such as kale and cabbage.

There are in fact six species of deer presently residing in the woods and hills of Britain. These are, in order of size, from largest to smallest:

1. red deer;
2. fallow deer;

3. sika deer;
4. roe deer;
5. Chinese water deer;
6. muntjac deer.

Despite a variety of differences in both the appearance and the habits of these deer, for the purpose of protecting growing trees and crops we can talk about them collectively, because they have common aspects of behaviour which the smallholder can effectively target to prevent damage occurring. However, it is worth pointing out that damage caused by the two smallest deer is negligible; chiefly because, in the case of the muntjac, it is content to graze on wild herbage, while the Chinese water deer does not appear in sufficient numbers to pose a real problem.

All types of deer are typically cautious animals; they have a very sensitive sense of smell and keen eyesight, which alert them to the presence of any strangers. For the most part they tend to lie up during the day, which is why the casual observer does not often see them. Sometimes they are active in the day, if the vegetation is dense enough to prevent them being spotted. Concealment and stillness are the deer's chief defensive strategies, but they will rapidly take flight if humans get close or if an unfamiliar noise startles them. Deer can be easily scared and this should be borne in mind when the smallholder is planning measures to tackle any problems associated with them. Woodland is the favoured home of the deer and a water source will invariably be located in the near vicinity.

Deer leave a variety of signs in the countryside indicative of their presence. As animals that habitually follow the same routes, well-worn pathways appear in the undergrowth and trees in a regular run can be worn by passing bodies. Debarking of trees and denuding of buds is another tell-tale sign. Belonging to the order Artiodactyla, which refers to hoofed animals,

Deer are a particular problem where woodland borders arable fields.

deer leave a clearly identifiable track in soft ground, similar in shape to that left by the domestic goat. Droppings may also be found, although these vary in appearance and size, depending on the species of deer that left them. Small areas of flattened vegetation, where the deer has been lying up during the day can often be observed.

There are two strategies for dealing with deer that the smallholder can choose from, these are:

1. To place some form of protection around vulnerable trees and crops.
2. To scare the deer away from these vulnerable areas by utilizing deterrents.

The first strategy will require some form of fencing and the choice is between wire and electric fencing. Wire fencing is a significant initial cost, but has the advantage of being long lasting and creates an effective protective barrier.

However, it must be made high enough because deer are tremendous jumpers and will easily clear the standard-height, stockproof fencing. It is essential that deer fencing be of a sufficient height to put deer off attempting to jump it, in order to avoid those situations where deer have got caught in the fencing, usually by a hind leg when trying to leap over it. The resulting injuries can be painful and debilitating and, in the worst cases, necessitate the destruction of an otherwise healthy animal. Good deer fencing will be at least 2m high and the most common types are chain link, or 1m high stockproof fencing, topped with five strands of wire to bring it to the required height and drop boards to hold these strands taut. Whereas these fences provide a permanent boundary, electric fencing can be employed as a temporary barrier. It has the added advantage of being easy to put up and can even be moved from one site to another as required. In those cases where

Deer fencing should be 2m high.

Deer, like goats, will strip overhanging tree branches leaving a clear browse line.

there are not many trees that need to be protected from deer, there is the option of placing individual tree guards around them.

A deer stalker knows all too well how easy it is to scare deer into taking flight. The most fleeting glance, or slightest scent of a person, will send the deer speedily in the opposite direction. The sight, sound or smell of something that appears strange to them is all that is required to stop deer straying into those portions of land that the smallholder wishes to protect. With this in mind, deer deterrents have been designed which incorporate a flashlight and radio speaker, which is activated when a deer crosses their path, with the intention of startling it into making a retreat. These deterrents can easily be fixed to trees, fence posts or walls. Repeller ribbon is also sold as a deer deterrent, however, as it relies on reflecting light, it is ineffective during the hours of darkness and therefore only of limited use in this context.

It is worth mentioning some atypical behaviour of deer that has been attributed to a rise in numbers, combined with their location being close to urban areas. The most striking case of this in recent years occurred at Easterhouse in Glasgow. Up to 200 roe deer were recorded frequenting this large, impoverished council estate. Photographs were taken of deer standing alongside parked cars during the day, which is in stark contrast to their usual habit of concealing themselves. Being so close to the hustle and bustle of human activity may lead to some of these deer being more daring and less flighty than their counterparts living deep in the countryside. Such deer are more likely to enter gardens in search of food and, if a deterrent is employed, there is the possibility of the deer becoming accustomed to the light and noise it generates, in the same way that brown hares living on an Irish airport have learnt to ignore the rumbling noise of aeroplanes as they land and take off.

If relying on such a device, the smallholder in this situation should regularly monitor its effectiveness. When the numbers of deer reach the levels seen at Easterhouse there is clearly a need to reduce the population, however, this kind of deer management is a specialized activity that should only be undertaken by those who have undergone appropriate training. Meanwhile the objective of the smallholder should be to deter deer and nullify their destructive activities by protecting woodland and crops.

THE PREDATORY PESTS

Up to this point the animals that have been discussed are classified as pests, chiefly because they eat food destined for livestock, either in the form of bagged cereals or grass pasture, and they damage woodland and consume valuable vegetable crops. With the exception of disease transmission by rodents, these pests pose absolutely no threat in terms of causing injury to the smallholder's livestock. However, the following group of animals, known collectively as 'the predatory pests', are a problem precisely for the opposite reason. They have no interest in growing crops or bags of stored feed, but they will, if given the opportunity, kill and eat some of the animals that are to be found on nearly every smallholding.

Fortunately, in Britain we do not have the large predators that inhabit countries like Canada and America and even parts of northern Europe. Consequently, in this country only a small minority of livestock are vulnerable to attack and these are:

- poultry and fowl, especially growing chicks;
- new-born lambs and kids;
- sick lambs and cast sheep.

Furthermore, in the case of the last two groups, there is only one of Britain's small number of predatory mammals that is actually capable of causing harm and this is the fox. All the other predators that belong to the family Mustelidae are not a danger to anything other than poultry and fowl.

THE FOX

With its handsome red coat and doggish anatomy the country fox, which stands approximately 35cm high and weighs about 7kg, is a beautiful looking creature. Despite this the red fox is an animal that in many people's opinion, particularly poultry keepers and shepherds, is synonymous with cunning, villainy and bloodthirsty killing. There are others who claim that fox attacks on poultry and lambs are exaggerated and, in the case of the latter, they suggest that it is the weak or dying that are preyed upon. Attempts have even been made to justify those incidents where a fox has killed all the inhabitants of a chicken house and only taken one away, on the grounds that the excitable flapping of chicken wings in such a confined space confuses the fox to such an extent that it behaves quite irrationally and not according to its true nature. This, however, is scant compensation for either the chickens or their owner.

The only sensible position for the smallholder to adopt is to be aware of the real damage that foxes can inflict, based upon verifiable accounts, and guard against such episodes happening to the animals in his care. Without doubt the killing of livestock by predators is one of the most demoralizing and distressing events that the smallholder is likely to encounter.

The plain fact is that the fox is a stealthy and efficient hunter and will prey upon both farm and wild animals as the opportunity presents itself. The largest part of the

Foxes are not difficult animals to trap but, once caught, they cannot be released. STV INTERNATIONAL

country fox's diet comprises: rats, voles, moles, mice and shrews, but poultry and fowl of all descriptions will be added to the diet if the fox can gain access to their houses or runs. Furthermore, it has been known for those foxes that have acquired a taste for such birds to actually spend nights in reconnaissance, looking for the slightest weakness in defences. Both healthy and sick lambs have been victims of the fox, particularly in the hill country. A study conducted in Linn County, Oregon, USA, revealed that foxes became very detrimental to poultry, game and young livestock when there was an over-abundance of them in farming areas, or a scarcity of their preferred food of rabbits and mice. Therefore, given the right circumstances the fox can prove to be a very real threat, which the smallholder should be aware of and not underestimate.

The fox has acute senses of hearing, sight and smell, which helps it to detect quarry and alerts it to the presence of any danger nearby. As any huntsman will testify, the fox possesses rapid reactions, quick thinking and a great deal of stamina when it is evading a pursuer. It is an animal of considerable athleticism and can jump tremendous heights and scale walls. Generally it chooses to make its home below ground; consequently it is an able,

though not overly keen digger, and often opts to widen rabbit burrows or share badger setts in order to save on the amount of digging required to fashion a home. In a similar way, it sometimes utilizes small caverns that occur naturally in mounds of rocks as a rudimentary but very effective shelter. This is often the case in Scotland where such abodes are referred to as cairns. Foxes have also been found living in disused drains, derelict outbuildings and under sheds.

The fox is therefore adept at squeezing its body through small openings and, much like the traditional working terrier, will contort and bend its body at remarkable angles to negotiate its way through or under obstacles when there is sufficient incentive. This is one of the reasons why they can pose such a threat to poultry that is not adequately housed. A good guide for the smallholder to bear in mind is that a poultry house or run cannot be deemed secure if a terrier can find its way in. This is because a fox will invariably be able to go wherever a terrier can go as they share similar anatomical features; namely, a deep narrow chest set upon short legs.

Foxes are typically most active during the hours of darkness and this is the period when vulnerable livestock are most at risk.

These are examples of a fox's chief target on a smallholding.

When food is scarce the fox will be tempted to hunt in broad daylight in areas where it has sufficient cover and a clear way of escape. They are territorial creatures and mark their boundaries with a distinctive and odorous scent. A family comprising a dog and one or two vixens will establish territories of between 100 acres in suburban areas to 2,500 acres in the hills, which they stoutly defend against any strange incomers of their own species.

This type of behaviour has given rise to the theory that it may be best to allow the resident foxes to remain on the land which they have adopted as their own, so that they can ward off any vagrant foxes. It was found that when landowners removed the two or three established foxes from their grounds they then had to deal with a succession of vagrant foxes, numbering twenty to thirty times that of the initial residents. Consequently, this is one way in which the fox may prove to be an ally to the smallholder. Another is by preying upon mice, stoats, voles and, most vitally, rats. During the period when rabbits were scarce due to myxomatosis, one fox was observed killing an impressive sixty-seven rats in one year.

The signs that a fox will leave indicating that it is in the area include: dog-like impressions of pads in soft ground, strands of red or reddish brown hair caught in the barbs of fences, scattered feathers or fur indicative of the killing of quarry, food remains and droppings, known as scats.

The most obvious way to avoid fox predation is to protect vulnerable livestock. There is an old country saying: 'Foxes carry no keys', which emphasizes this point; in other words, if chickens, ducks, turkeys or geese are securely shut in strong, well-made houses at night they cannot be killed by a fox. Prior to the 1940s, many poultry keepers in America were accustomed to leaving their hens out unprotected overnight; however, when they were persuaded to adopt the routine of shutting their birds in purpose-built sheds before it got dark, the positive results soon became apparent as no loss of birds was registered. During two visits to a ranch a fox had killed seventeen hens but, as the farmer started to confine his chickens to a shed as soon as the light faded, there was no opportunity for the fox to attack his birds.

Generally poultry keepers in this country have always been more disciplined about putting their poultry away in a secure environment, recognizing, quite rightly, that it is a fundamental responsibility of any livestock keeper to ensure that his

Anatomically a fox resembles a working terrier and shares its capacity for getting into unusual and confined spaces.

Good quality timber and bolts top and bottom, make the door of this shed fox- and badger-proof. DOMESTIC FOWL TRUST

animals are given adequate protection from predators. Placing poultry, fowl or game in insecure, ramshackle buildings or failing to exercise the diligence to close them in before it gets dark, is to gamble with their lives and provides the fox with an irresistible invitation to mount a raid. Other measures that can be taken to protect birds from foxes include: putting up electric poultry netting, or a permanent electric fence around their run, or confining them within small impenetrable runs, usually constructed of weld mesh wire.

The second most common animal associated with fox predation is the new-born or ailing lamb. One of the most practical ways to avoid this is to lamb inside outbuildings, or within a corral of hurdles or square bales placed near to the smallholder's house, where people will constantly be at hand. This has the added benefit of sheltering the lambs from any adverse weather, as well as the smallholder being on the spot should any assistance with

the birthing be required. As smallholdings do not encompass the vast tracts of land, or contain the density of livestock that the average farmer or hill shepherd has to contend with, it is quite feasible to utilize some form of shelter located near to a dwelling for lambing.

There are an assortment of tools produced to keep the fox at bay. These include wildlife deterrents, designed to scare the naturally cautious fox into running away by emitting a loud noise, accompanied by a flash of light. However, the intelligent fox is likely to grow accustomed to such a device if it remains constantly fixed in the same position; it is therefore worthwhile routinely moving it. Live capture traps are also available, but these can be expensive and the wary fox can prove to be a difficult animal to trap. Should the smallholder succeed in trapping a fox he is then faced with the problem of disposing of it, which requires the use of a firearm.

Rearing lambs inside is an ideal way to avoid fox problems.

Without question, the most effective fox deterrent is a dog, or group of dogs that are regularly walked around the smallholder's fields and allowed the freedom to meander in and out of the barns and livestock pens. The dogs that I keep on my smallholding regard it as their duty to guard the grounds and clearly derive a great deal of satisfaction from doing so. They have, on numerous occasions, scared foxes away, either by simply barking at them or chasing after them. I have not yet encountered a country fox that will opt to confront a dog instead of taking flight immediately. In fact, the mere presence of a dog is sufficient to stop a fox getting too close. The dogs with the most instinctive feel for this type of duty are the sheepdog breeds and terriers.

THE MUSTELIDS

The largest group of predatory mammals in Britain belong to the family Mustelidae or, in layman's terms, the weasel family. The members of the family that we are particularly interested in are: the weasel, stoat, polecat, domestic ferret and mink. Although the much larger badger also belongs to the family, it differs so dramatically in habit from the others that it shall be discussed separately. Essentially the weasel, stoat, polecat, ferret and mink possess the same anatomical shape. They each have long, narrow, lithe bodies set upon short legs, which results in a distinctive arching of the back when they move, although they tend to straighten out more when they are running at full speed. They are all determined and ruthless hunters, capable of killing animals much bigger than themselves; they also have a characteristic way of killing their prey that is easy to identify and involves a deep bite, delivered to the base or nape of the neck. They have a certain degree of athletic prowess as they can swim, climb and jump and such talents, combined with their obstinate nature, rapid digging action and teeth that can make holes in standard chicken wire, make them very difficult pests to exclude.

In the past, all members of the group have been subject to determined and rigorous control, chiefly by gamekeepers and to a lesser extent poultry keepers; consequently, the concentration of mustelids throughout the country is not as great as it used to be. Nevertheless, any of them that gains entrance into a bird house or run is likely to leave a trail of devastation in its wake, which is guaranteed to distress and outrage the keeper. The most common and effective method of control is trapping, using either tunnel or live capture traps.

Although the various members of this family, which share so much in common, do differ from one another in some vital respects, most notably: size, fur colour and the level of threat they pose to the smallholder's birds.

Weasel

Measuring between 15 and 22cm long and weighing as little as 45g, the weasel is the smallest of carnivorous creatures. Despite this, it has been referred to as the fiercest and most aggressive animal in the world for its size. It is certainly an active, courageous and pertinacious animal that is cunning and persistent when pursuing prey. This is typically portrayed in the way it attracts birds by so called 'dancing', which involves running in circles after its tail, interspersed with a series of bounds, leaps and hops. The bird watching this erratic display of behaviour often becomes so fascinated that it advances dangerously close to the weasel, which duly pounces upon the bird. It is an accomplished example of both luring prey and catching it completely off guard. The weasel's main and favoured diet consists of mice and voles, which they are small enough to chase into the tunnels and burrows they hide in. Young rabbits, small birds, rats, bird's eggs and frogs will also be eaten and, on very rare occasions, a weasel has been observed killing a hare. Once an animal has been killed, the weasel will drag it off to the shelter of a den to eat it, always starting with the head first.

While hunting they will cover an area of no less than three, but rarely exceeding nine acres, most commonly at night, although it has been suggested that they are often abroad during the day but go undetected because of their minuscule size and swift movement. Their dark brown coat can merge seamlessly with the surrounding

If handling a member of the weasel family, the smallholder should wear thick leather gauntlets and hold it in the same way as this ferret.

vegetation, and grass that is no more than 25mm high is tall enough to conceal a weasel. The weasel will usually make a home utilizing the burrow of one of its victims but is equally happy to squeeze into any nook or cranny in dry stone walls. Weasels can be found wherever there is a suitable supply of food; as they primarily feast upon mice this means nearly every environment in Britain; they have also been known to occupy farm buildings and penetrate hay stacks so that they can pursue rodents. It has been calculated that a family of weasels could realistically kill as many as

A weasel can squeeze through the small gaps in this chicken wire.

2,000 mice in one year. Their value as mice killers has been long recognized; during Saxon times weasels were actually kept by households in order to catch mice entering their buildings. Despite being so ferocious towards their prey, weasels are apparently quite easy to tame, as demonstrated in quite recent publications such as Phil Drabble's *A Weasel in my Meat Safe* and Francis Pitt's *Animals of Britain*.

In many respects the weasel is an invisible occupant of the land because it leaves no discernible signs or tracks indicative of its presence and, were it not for rare glimpses of the creature, we would remain totally ignorant of its whereabouts. Being not much thicker than a man's finger, the weasel has proved itself capable of getting into places that people thought were secure. Bird fanciers who have constructed fine aviaries have reported finding canaries and budgerigars killed and still been unable to ascertain how a predator gained entrance through the thick, narrow meshed aviary wire. The ability to squeeze through cracks and gaps, which are often easily overlooked because they are so small, is one of the weasel's greatest assets.

Consequently, a very careful eye needs to be cast over chicken and duck housing, to ensure that it can withstand the scrutinizing survey of a hungry weasel; if there are any gaps through which a finger can comfortably be poked they should be covered without delay. However, weasel attacks on full-grown hens and ducks are quite rare and it is usually chicks during the early weeks of life that are most vulnerable. One year I observed a family of weasels living in the border of my field, which was less than 200m from the duck and chicken houses and pens; yet I never lost one of my birds to them. The fact that I did not encounter any problems is probably because I always shut my birds in secure houses before it gets dark and only let them out when it gets light, thus ensuring that they are out of harm's way during the most dangerous hours. An abundance of mice, voles and shrews in the field for the weasels to prey upon, may also have been a contributing factor.

The weasel's fondness for these animals and other rodent pests led the writers of *The Standard Cyclopaedia of Modern Agriculture* to state that it is a creature whose practical importance is indisputable and, therefore, it should not be molested. While the density of the weasel population remains at its present level, the smallholder will probably find that this is a sentiment that he can share. This fact is highlighted by the absence of any mention of weasels as a pest in contemporary books concerning the care and management of domestic fowl, authored by experts on the subject.

Stoat

The stoat is, in many respects, a larger version of a weasel, measuring from 26–29.5cm long and weighing between 210 and 320g, depending on gender. It has a similar reddish brown coat with a white underbelly, tinged with yellow. There is however, a distinctive difference between the two, which is the chief means of telling them apart and this is the stoat's black tip to its tail. The stoat also changes colour from reddish brown to white in the winter. If the winter weather is unusually mild, or alternates between cold and warm, the coat will remain red or become mottled respectively.

The stoat has been referred to as 'the terror of the countryside'; it is reputed to pursue its prey so relentlessly that it becomes exhausted and seemingly reaches a stage where it is unable to flee its pursuer any longer. This apparent giving up is attributed to the stoat's presence, instilling a paroxysm of fear. Its main diet consists of: rats, mice, voles, rabbits, leverets and game birds and the stoat will occasionally raid poultry yards, where it will not only kill chickens, but also carry off eggs which it relishes.

Although the stoat cannot fit through spaces as small as the weasel, it can dig and climb at great speed, which makes it difficult to keep out of a standard poultry run. However, it is largely nocturnal in habit and is unlikely to attempt poultry raids during daylight hours, choosing to avoid attracting attention from people or dogs. It has a considerable home range of between 40 and 800 acres – depending on how abundant the food supply is – and systematically hunts over the entire range by dividing it up into sections and spending a couple of days hunting each section.

The stoat can be found throughout Britain, but owing to the systematic control delivered by gamekeepers, does not occur in sufficient numbers anywhere to make it a primary pest. By nature it is extremely inquisitive, typified by such behaviour as running away from a person into the cover of the nearest hedge, only to reappear moments later to scrutinize the person that it fled from in the first place. This curiosity makes it an easy animal to trap and shoot. Like the weasel it leaves few clues of its presence and will make a home out of an old rabbit warren, hollow tree or tiny cavern among rocks.

Despite doing great service to man by destroying an assortment of rodents, the stoat also has the capacity to rapidly decimate the smallholder's flock of birds and should therefore be carefully guarded against. The measures that should be implemented to deal with the threat of stoat predation are the same as those employed against the weasel.

Polecat

The polecat is totally different in colour to the stoat and weasel, having a lush sable coat. The muzzle and head often have indiscriminate white markings, but the most distinctive feature of the polecat is a black band that covers both eyes and gives the impression that the animal is wearing a mask, which has been labelled the 'robber's mask'. The polecat is also considerably bigger than the stoat, measuring approximately 65cm in length and typically weighing around 1.5kg. As is the case with all mustelids, the feature of sexual dimorphism means that the male polecat, known as the hob, is always quite a lot larger, even sometimes double the size of the female, commonly referred to as a jill.

Owing to this increase in size, the polecat is not able to squeeze through the tiny spaces that a weasel and stoat can, however, it has the ability to elongate its body in such a way that it can pass through holes that are a mere 8cm in diameter. Although it is not as graceful a climber as the stoat and weasel it will, without faltering, ascend chicken wire as if it were a ladder and is adept at utilizing objects such as boxes, bins, pallets and bales as steps, even jumping from one to another. It can also quickly excavate a half-circle hole of sufficient size for it to fit under a fence and, if a polecat finds weak or rotten wood preventing it getting where it wants to go, it will use its long, sharp teeth

Although slightly darker in colour, the wild polecat closely resembles the domesticated ferret pictured here.

and exceptionally strong neck to rip it out of the way.

The polecat is the least common of the weasel family and is most likely to be encountered in parts of Wales, where they establish and patrol a range of anything between a couple of hundred and a few thousand acres. As a solitary animal the polecat will mark the boundaries of its territory with a pungent odour, secreted from glands located below the tail. It may also release this characteristic noxious smell in response to being startled, scared or hurt. The polecat is a skilful hunter that can catch its prey both above and below ground, where it relies primarily on the senses of scent and sound to detect and pursue the prey animal. Its main diet is composed of: rabbits, mice and rats and to a lesser extent fish, frogs and lizards. Unfortunately for the smallholder, it also has a taste for poultry, fowl and game birds and will turn to these at times when other food is scarce.

The polecat is essentially nocturnal in habit and favours keeping to the cover of trees, hedges and thick vegetation when on the move. It does move along established trails leaving narrow pathways of no more than 8cm. Occasionally, long cylindrical droppings measuring around 30mm in length and 5mm thick can be found, as well as food remnants consisting almost entirely of bone, as the polecat routinely consumes a large portion of fur and feather. With its dense fur coat, the polecat copes well with the cold weather and is usually content with shelter in a hollow tree, disused burrow, little cave in rocks and walls and, very occasionally, a badger sett which it is able to share, thanks to the courtesy of the much larger occupant. Being keen on comfort it will invariably line these varied occupancies with long grass, bits of stubble and animal fur, so that it has a cosy nest in which to sleep which, like all mustelids, it enjoys doing a great deal.

The actual name polecat is thought to spring from a French term meaning 'chicken cat', which refers to its capacity to create mayhem in a poultry house or yard. No polecat, if it is given just the slightest chance, will pass by birds without doing a great deal of harm. Should it enter a house or run where the birds have no opportunity of escape, the polecat will kill or maim bird after bird; ducks that seek refuge in ponds are not safe either because the polecat is an accomplished swimmer, following close on the heels of the mink and otter. Consequently, in an area where polecats are known to reside, the smallholder must exercise constant vigilance. The most effective measures that he can take include: ensuring the birds have suitably designed housing, erecting electric netting and employing live capture traps. Fortunately, polecats only pose a problem in certain regions and, even then, occur in such meagre numbers that they are considered to be only an occasional pest to those who have agricultural or sporting interests. It is worth bearing in mind when dealing with polecats, that they appear in Schedule 6 of the Wildlife and Countryside Act of 1981, which gives clear guidelines on how they are to be treated.

Ferret

The ferret is so similar to the polecat that the two are often confused, or erroneously thought to be the same animal. In fact, unlike the wild polecat, the ferret is a domesticated animal and has been such for many centuries. While the origin of the ferret is obscure, it is well documented that people in Britain have used the animal for approximately 800 years to catch rabbits and rats. It may appear strange that an animal that is domesticated and has played such a constant and prominent role in catching some of the most numerous and destructive of pests, should itself be identified as a potential pest. Clearly this is a matter requiring some clarification.

Probably more ferrets are kept in Britain today than at any other time, mostly due to the fact that, as well as those who keep ferrets for their traditional role as rabbit catchers, there are an increasing number of people who keep ferrets solely as pets. According to both the RSPCA and SSPCA, with whom I have worked closely over many years rehoming ferrets, there has recently been a marked rise in the number of ferrets found wandering free. Obviously some of these will have escaped from weak cages, or they may have been lost during the course of their work pursuing rabbits; however, some are simply being abandoned in the countryside and left to fend for themselves because they are no longer wanted. It is the lost, wandering ferret that can be a definite pest to the smallholder, because it will be in search of food and, unlike its wild relatives, does not have a fear of people; it will quite brazenly walk onto a property at any time of the day or night. It is this, in conjunction with its unpredictable behaviour and the fierce hunting talents of the stoat, weasel and polecat, that makes the loose ferret such a danger.

I witnessed the destruction caused by a ferret when it gained entrance to a duck house. The ferret was a small jill and killed four ducks outright and severely injured two others, one of which was a drake that had tried to put up a fight, but to no avail. Had the keeper not heard the commotion and quickly entered the shed he would have lost all of his birds. Ironically, he was able to pick the jill up without getting bitten and it was obvious to him that the ferret was used to being handled. I remember another occasion when I was asked to help at a house where a ferret had killed two guinea pigs and eaten one and was peacefully resting in their cage. I retrieved him and gave him a permanent home and he proved to be a lovely character, despite the fact that in a certain situation he had showed himself to be nothing more than a cold-blooded killer. Clearly ferret attacks like these are devastating because the animal kills far in excess of what it actually needs to eat.

Consequently, the smallholder keeping poultry and fowl should make provision to ensure that his birds are kept safe from attacks, whether they are attempted during the day or at night. The measures he should implement are the same as those for dealing with polecats and, in addition, he may be able to pick up any stray ferret that crosses his path because, more often than not, they are quite tame. Of course those who are nervous about handling a ferret and worried they might get bitten, can wear a pair of thick leather gloves or gauntlets.

Correct identification of the animal is obviously essential. Although sizes vary greatly depending upon gender, breeding and diet, the ferret typically possesses a long lithe body set on short legs, has a wedge-shaped head set upon a thick neck at one end and a tail, measuring approximately half its body length at the other; in between the two is a long vertebral

In these four photographs, one of my ferrets shows why it is difficult to prevent members of the weasel family from gaining access to barns and runs, as it demonstrates its ability to climb up stone walls, use wire like a ladder and squeeze itself through small holes.

This ferret shows the outline typical of the weasel family.

column that results in the characteristic arching of the back in the mid-section. In colour the ferret can either be the traditional white-coloured albino with red eyes, a dark sable with a mask, just like a polecat, or a ginger-coloured version of a polecat. The only possible confusion with identification arises between the polecat ferret and the wild polecat because they have such similar and characteristic markings, although the wild polecat tends to be darker. For those who live in regions where polecats do not reside this is obviously not an issue, however, if the animal is seen during the day, does not flee or show excessive wariness of people and responds to the human voice, it will more than likely be a polecat ferret.

Mink

There were no mink found in the British countryside until the 1930s, when specimens of the North American mink began to escape from fur farms, first in Devon and later in other parts of the country. During the 1960s the wild mink flourished and became firmly established, due to the lack of any indigenous predatory animals to prey upon it. With nothing to fear, it quickly earned a reputation as a notorious pest, guilty of damaging fish stocks, game and domestic poultry.

Being particularly fond of water and a very capable swimmer the mink will always be found fairly near to a river, stream, brook, ditch or even pond, if it is of sufficient size. At such a location the mink, being a solitary animal, will mark a territory sometimes extending several miles along a river bank.

Within this territory it will have a number of dens to shelter in; typically these are burrows dug into the river bank, often underneath trees.

The mink is considerably bigger and heavier than the stoat, weasel and polecat and measures from 45–75cm and weighs between 2 and 3kg. Being so fond of the water it acquires the bulk of its food from the wetland environment and this includes: ducklings, moorhens, mallards, coots and various species of fish. It will also predate poultry and domestic fowl, as well as turkeys and geese; losses of this nature recorded during a fifteen-year period amounted to several hundred birds.

The mink is an intense dark brown in colour with a white chin, throat and sometimes belly. As cautious animals that favour keeping to cover, they are rarely seen, despite being active during the day. Like most of the weasel clan they travel along well worn, established trails, moving along at a gallop with the distinctive arched gait and sometimes leaving impressions of pads featuring five toes in soft ground.

There are concerted efforts being made at present by river authorities and conservation groups to control the mink; their success quite obviously reduces the risk of the smallholder suffering any loss of birds to mink predation. Additional precautions can include: placing wire mesh fencing, with squares no larger than 30mm, around poultry houses and runs. A strand of electric fencing, set halfway up and 50mm away from the fence is a further deterrent. Strategically located live capture traps can also prove useful, due to the mink's curious nature.

Weld mesh, as used in this run, is a greater deterrent to predators than standard chicken wire. DOMESTIC FOWL TRUST

Badger

In previous years I have been fortunate enough to do a lot of badger watching and there is no doubt how interesting the habits and behaviour of this distinctive looking animal are, with its black and white striped face and silvery grey coat. Although it is related to the weasel tribe, it is by no means as fierce a predator as the stoat, weasel, polecat or mink and survives largely on earthworms, fruit, acorns, slugs and bulbs and only occasionally preys upon: voles, mice, moles, hedgehogs and young rabbits.

Being nocturnal in habit the badger rests in its large underground dwelling, known as a sett, during the day. Setts consist of an extensive labyrinth of interconnected tunnels, commonly terminating in holes on the surface and are typically dug into the side of wooded hills, embankments and ditches. One sett that was excavated in England was found to conceal an astonishing ninety tunnels stretching for more than 300m. Consequently, the home of the badger is considered one of the most easily recognized dwellings of British mammals. In addition to its size, a sett usually has at least twenty holes and is clearly identified by huge mounds of excavated material as badgers are in the habit of regularly tipping out their substantial bedding of: dry grass, straw, bracken, moss, fern and dry leaves.

There will also be footprints, about the size of a medium-sized dog, strands of coarse black and white hair and well-trodden paths leading to water for drinking and latrines, where the build-up of droppings forms small mounds. Apparently some of these paths date back hundreds of years and continue to be habitually travelled by badgers. Trees located near to a sett may also exhibit small scratch marks where a badger has sharpened its claws, and sycamore trees are sometimes debarked to a height of 40cm by a badger searching for the sweet tasty sap. Although the badger is not an animal that hibernates, it does sensibly remain below ground during bouts of inclement weather.

The badger is a stout, short-legged creature weighing approximately 18kg and measuring up to 80cm long. They have very distinctive black and white facial markings and, as gregarious animals, live in communes with family dynasties often occupying the same sett.

Very occasionally a badger will attack poultry; when this happens it is called a rogue badger, in order to emphasize that such behaviour is not typical of the species. In fact, such attacks have been attributed to either: food scarcity, an old badger or one seeking an easy meal. The vast majority of badgers will never touch poultry and a well-designed house, with secure latches that the birds are put in at night, will mitigate this problem. Another charge laid at the badger's door is the unintentional spread of bovine tuberculosis, which has serious ramifications for cattle that become infected and the keeper who either wants to move, sell or breed from them. Badgers are protected by law and it is an offence to capture or kill a badger, unless a special licence has been granted on the grounds that the animal is causing substantial damage to crops, killing poultry or hindering the use of agricultural machinery as a result of extensive digging. The smallholder can avoid problems by ensuring badgers cannot access his buildings and make use of electric fencing to stop them coming into contact with his livestock.

AVIAN PESTS

Just like the mammals we have discussed, some species of bird that are common throughout Britain, can be a real nuisance to the smallholder by eating seed, destroying crops, stealing eggs and costly animal feed and even occasionally harming livestock. There has been an ongoing battle for centuries between farmers and birds, both in Britain and America. There are records of small farms, particularly in America during the nineteenth century, being brought to the brink of ruin by marauding flocks of birds, hovering over their crops like locusts. Today birds remain a hindrance to the productivity of the smallholding, with members of the crow family being among the worst offenders. However, I shall start by looking at the bird which has earned the reputation as the worst obvious pest of agriculture, apart from insects, bacteria and viruses: the wood pigeon, whose suppression was traditionally viewed as a matter of urgency.

The Wood Pigeon

This is the largest and most common of the four species of British pigeon and is well known throughout all parts of the country. As its name implies, the bird was initially an inhabitant of woodlands, but has moved into towns and onto farmland in its constant search for food. This food consists of: seed and grain of all kinds, peas, beans, turnips, cabbages, lettuce, cauliflower, carrots and berries. The wood pigeon also eats weeds and weed foliage, just as readily as they eat the seed and leaves of cultivated plants but chemical weedkillers have markedly reduced the amount of weed foliage in crops. This reduction in weeds, combined with more intensive farming practices, increases the harm done by pigeons. In the countryside, its extreme shyness makes it very difficult to approach, although in many London parks it displays absolutely no fear of humans. The typical wariness of the rural dwelling wood pigeon secures it comparative safety and makes it a difficult bird to control.

ABOVE: Vegetables such as these are an irresistible temptation for pigeons.

RIGHT: This shows the size and colouring of pigeons.

It tends to desert northern regions during the extreme cold weather and in winter goes about in large flocks, whereas in summer it is usually seen in pairs. The wood pigeon is approximately 41cm in length, bluish grey in colour with a pink chest and black tips to wings and tail feathers. In the past the wood pigeon was known as the ring dove, which referred to small white patches located on either side of the neck. In flight it is easily recognized by two conspicuous white bars across the wings.

There are three things the smallholder can do to prevent the damage commonly caused by wood pigeons:

• Use horticultural netting to protect at-risk crops;
• Place bird scarers which rely on noise, light or movement to frighten the birds;
• Shoot them with an air rifle. If this method is selected it is vital that the smallholder ensures he is correctly identifying the birds he is targeting.

The feral pigeon can also be found on smallholdings and farms throughout the country. It is smaller than the wood pigeon, measuring only 33cm in length and is bluish grey with multi-coloured wings, a white rump and black bars on either side of the neck. Formerly inhabitants of dovecots, built by man so that the pigeons could be easily harvested for food, the feral pigeon is most at home roosting in outbuildings and can cause a considerable mess with their droppings. Its diet consists of seed and any livestock feed or scraps it can find. The chief way to deal with feral pigeons is with an air rifle when they are roosting. It is also claimed that it is possible to catch them by hand during the night, if all sources of light are blocked out.

THE CROW FAMILY

The word crow is often used as a general term for any member belonging to the Corvidae family that includes: the magpie, carrion and hooded crow, jackdaw and rook.

The Magpie

The magpie is probably one of the easiest birds to recognize, because of its long tail and distinctive black and white colouring. When not in flight the white bars on the wings form the basic shape of the letter 'V' across its back. It also has a white belly and black beak. Although it is typically long, this is largely due to the length of the tail and the actual body of the bird is not as big as you would expect.

As a thief the magpie has few rivals and one of the crimes it is particularly accomplished at is stealing poultry eggs. It appears to have the ability to identify the routine of the smallholder, where and when the hens lay their eggs, and the window of opportunity they have to grab them before they are collected. I have observed a magpie sitting on top of a fencepost near to my poultry house, just waiting for the familiar cackle of the hen announcing to the world that it has laid an egg. It swoops in as soon as the hen is off the nest and scoops up the egg, which it relishes eating, often not too far from the scene of the crime. Abandoned eggshells, still retaining their oval shape but with a hole pecked into them about the size of a two pence piece and with the contents completely removed, is a typical remnant left courtesy of a magpie. Although clearly audacious, the magpie is equally wary and has the most acute eyesight that alerts it to any danger. Consequently it always keeps people at a safe distance and is very easily scared off. As well as stealing eggs, a magpie will kill young chicks if it is given the chance.

In order to prevent the loss of eggs, the following measures can be taken. Fowl and poultry can be left shut in their houses until all eggs have been laid and collected; however, this requires large houses and is only really feasible if the birds lay their eggs early in the day, which often they do not. Baited Larsen traps can be employed to distract the attention of the magpie and catch it. Regular checking of the nest box and collection of eggs can also put a

The Larsen trap is a traditional tool for dealing with magpies. Note the distinctive black and white markings of the magpie.
STV INTERNATIONAL

Like rabbits, pigeons can be a source of food to supplement home-grown vegetables.

magpie off its stride and deprive it of any opportunities to steal. When only small flocks are kept, an enclosed run may prove to be an adequate solution and such runs are always recommended for the protection of chicks.

The Carrion and Hooded Crows

The carrion and hooded crows are discussed together because they exhibit identical behaviour as they are sub-species of the same species. The only differences between them, apart from their names, are their colouring and the places in Britain where they reside. The carrion crow is what we think of as a traditional crow, being entirely black in plumage as well as in the bill, beak, legs, feet and claws; whereas the hooded crow has only a black head, throat, wing tops and tail, the remainder of the body and the underside of the wings being grey. The carrion crow is resident in England, Wales, southern, central and north east Scotland, whereas the hooded is a resident of west Scotland, the Highlands and Ireland.

Early historical records reveal that the crow has long been considered a despicable predator and King Henry VIII put a bounty on the crow along with its relatives, the chough and the rook. The carrion and hooded crows remain the most destructive and troublesome of crows, as they will not only feed upon dead animals but also prey upon the sick, injured, dying and young. Furthermore, according to reputed naturalist Brian Vesey-Fitzgerald in his book entitled, *Town Fox, Country Fox*, in parts of Scotland the hooded crow is considered to be a greater menace to lambs than the fox. They have also been known to peck into the taut stomach of sheep that are cast and withdraw parts of the intestines through the hole their sharp beak has made, while the helpless sheep is immobile. However,

as any driver will confirm, they also find a lot of their food in the form of road kill and eat such things as: spiders, snails, wild and domestic birds' eggs and insects such as wireworms, caterpillars and moths. Both these crows are great opportunists and will make the most of any free sources of food that the smallholder unwittingly presents them with. A typical example of their opportunism took place on the Canadian duck nesting marshes during the 1930s, when colonies of nearby crows accounted for just over 30 per cent of the season's laying.

The two crows are suspicious of everything that is strange and new and will take flight if a person advances too close to them, although they are by no means secretive in habit and are quite content to be watched from a distance. They are not birds that are easily scared and seem quite unperturbed by motor vehicles speeding past them when they are feasting on a dead animal by the side of the road. They have a familiar and distinctive call which has been described as 'caw, caw' becoming a prolonged 'c-a-a-w' when a warning is issued by a bird doing sentinel duty. The crows deposit pellets, often on the top of fence posts, which are made up of the regurgitated indigestible parts of animals such as bone, teeth and fur. They have few natural enemies, as they are arboreal by habit and roost and nest in trees inaccessible to most animals. A group of crows will mob any stranger and in particular an owl, even if it is a plastic one.

Crows can be reduced in number by shooting them with an air rifle or by using a Larsen trap, baited with carrion of some kind, such as paunched rabbit. Timing is crucial and control measures should be undertaken prior to the lambing season. Lambing and the treatment of sick or injured animals in outbuildings or shelters is another way of preventing problems.

The Rook

This is the commonest British bird referred to as a crow and has a better reputation than the other crows. In certain situations it can actually aid agriculture and farming by eating harmful pests and grubs where the ground is used as pasture. The rook's diet is decidedly mixed and a twelve-month study of 330 rooks, conducted in 1894, was able to analyse precisely what the birds were eating: 58 per cent of their diet was composed of cereal grain and husks, followed by insect grubs at 23 per cent, miscellaneous at 12 per cent and finally potatoes at 7 per cent. In 1907, Professor Theobold, from studies conducted in Kent, placed injurious insects and insect larvae as the rook's primary food, particularly in the months of June and July. The Dutch authority on the subject, Professor Ritaema Bos found that rooks would eat weak voles, eggs and the young of small birds, earthworms and insects.

Extensive studies led to the view that the rook is neither wholly harmful nor entirely beneficial, but opinion varied as to which one predominated. When insect pests are numerous the benefit conferred is large, but when they are not the farmer and grower are justified in keeping down numbers because rooks can do substantial damage, by devouring sprouting and half-ripe grain and have been known to dig up and peck at potatoes. Bird scarers of various designs and air weapons can be employed to prevent such damage.

Rooks are present throughout all parts of Britain, measure 46–50cm in length and have a black plumage with a characteristic bluish sheen. The long powerful beak is slightly curved downwards. One very marked feature is the bare, white patch around the base of the beak on the adult bird and this, together with their gregarious habit – they are most often seen in sizable flocks – are the easiest way to recognize them. The flight is easy compared to that of the carrion crow, which is heavy and clumsy. Rooks build their nests in company among the top branches of tall trees and the nests are made chiefly of intertwined twigs lined with mud, wool and fibre.

Rooks are likely to be found where there is an abundance of trees, such as these surrounding the chicken house.

The Jackdaw

Jackdaws are the crows often seen disappearing down people's chimneys, where they will construct a nest of twigs if given the chance. They are smaller than both rooks and carrion crows, measuring only 33cm in length and they lack the white markings of the magpie. The jackdaw is found in both town and country throughout Britain and lives in flocks that will unite as one to defend any of their number that is being attacked. In appearance the jackdaw, like the rook, has a glossy black plumage with a bluish tinge and has the added distinctive marking of a silver grey nape.

Jackdaws have been written about as chiefly beneficial, destroying large numbers of wireworms and other insects and removing parasites from the backs of stock. Occasionally they do harm by damaging cherries, taking eggs and filching food from poultry. To combat these actions the smallholder has the choice of using fruit cages, horticultural grade bird netting and automatic, on-demand poultry feeders.

The Jay

This handsome relative of the crow is about 33cm long and is readily distinguished by its black moustache and the blue markings on its tail and wings. The bulky, cup-shaped nest is made of twigs and roots, lined with grass and usually placed in a tree fork or among bushes. Jays are essentially woodland birds and their mixed diet consists of: acorns, beech mast and other fruit, or tree seeds, together with mice, nestlings, eggs, especially those of blackbirds, slugs, snails and insects. They are a pest to the fruit grower, damaging many apples and plums. The jay also ravages nuts and peas and both the fruit grower and gardener should take measures to check the activity of this bird. These include providing some form of crop protection, using a device to scare them off the crops, or shooting them, which is probably the most difficult option owing to the bird's instinctive caution and distrust of humans.

LEGAL ASPECTS OF AVIAN PEST CONTROL

With regard to the control of avian pests, the most important article of legislation is the Wildlife and Countryside Act of 1981, which highlights the protection provided for wild birds. Essentially, it is an offence to kill, injure or take any wild bird, with the exception of those identified in Schedule 2 of the Act. These include: the wood pigeon, feral pigeon, magpie, carrion and hooded crow, rook, jackdaw and jay. The Act makes provision for the Department for the Environment, Food and Rural Affairs and the Scottish Executive to issue what is referred to as a general licence, which allows the killing of the aforementioned birds at all times of the year, if it can be proved that they are doing serious damage to: crops, vegetables, fruit, growing timber, foodstuffs for livestock and fish stocks. Even then the actions to control these birds may only be undertaken by the occupier of the land, or somebody acting on his behalf, and he must ensure that only approved methods of control are employed. Included amongst these are the use of air weapons and Larsen traps, which have been referred to in this chapter. It is an offence to use: poisoned bait, a bow, crossbow, smoke, gas or a spring trap of any description on birds.

chapter three

Managing the Smallholding as a Form of Pest Control

There is no doubt that preventing the unwanted attention of animals categorized as pests is preferable to remedial action, or the culling of pests after they have caused damage and destruction. It is a source of great annoyance to any smallholder to realize that a simple action, whether it is the repair of a building or the prompt disposal of rubbish, could have stopped mice, rats or a fox wreaking havoc.

A badly managed, untidy smallholding will attract the attention of marauding pests, because of the myriad of opportunities it presents for finding food and shelter. Consequently, one of the most effective measures that the smallholder can take to prevent pest associated problems, is simply to keep his land and buildings tidy and in a good state of repair. This will deter pests because there will be no reward, in terms of food, arising from their visits. Furthermore, the removal of vegetation and rubbish that would usually camouflage pests, will leave them exposed and in a position of vulnerability, which they would much rather avoid. Having a tidy smallholding also enables a person to notice the very first signs of pest damage, which will, in turn, lead to prompt action and the prevention of serious problems.

Admittedly the smallholder will have plenty of demands on his time. As a keeper of livestock and grower of fruit, vegetables and grain, there is a continuous cycle of tasks to perform; it is often easy to fail to put items away properly, or dump rubbish haphazardly with the intention of moving it at a later date, as it is considered less important than other pressing tasks. However, I have learnt by experience that tidying as you go is ultimately far easier and less time consuming than dealing with it at a later date, after pests have had a chance to rummage through it.

The fundamental principles upon which a well-managed smallholding is built are as follows.

Barns should be kept clean and tidy to help combat pests.

CAREFUL PLANNING

Every smallholder should spend time identifying and scrutinizing the potential his land and buildings have, so that he can designate to each a specific purpose that suits its size, location and structure. This will certainly help the smallholder avoid the mistakes I made, mainly due to my over-enthusiasm to experience everything the world of smallholding had to offer. The worst of these was overstocking with too many animals and having unrealistic expectations of what the land at my disposal could support and produce. I quickly discovered that it is more rewarding to keep fewer animals to a high standard, than have a lot in a poor to mediocre fashion. Every livestock keeper should remember that he is responsible for providing his animals with an adequate supply of nutritious food and water, a clean, safe place to live, where they have the freedom to move about, are sheltered from the weather and receive prompt treatment for any illness or injuries.

In a similar fashion, the essential tenets of cultivating the land, such as the application of feed and organic matter and the correct spacing of seeds and plants, should be adhered to. Consequently, the smallholder should ask himself:

- What can be housed and stored in the outbuildings at his disposal?
- Has he enough land to support all the animals he wants to keep?
- Is there a secure and convenient place to put vulnerable animals, for example, either young or sick, where they can be easily observed?
- What crops will grow in the environment in which he lives and the soil type he has?
- What is the best site for the specific crops he wants to grow?

A penned yard near to the house is ideal for raising young stock.

MAINTENANCE OF PROPERTY AND BUILDINGS

This is undertaken not simply for the appearance of the smallholding but, more vitally, to avoid providing pests with easy access to buildings and safe, concealed pathways to travel along to get to those buildings. Typical tasks include: cutting down vegetation growing by outbuildings, replacing or repairing rotten doors and doorways, filling and covering any holes and re-cementing loose render, which is particularly important in stone and granite walls.

ESTABLISHING A DAILY ROUTINE

Animals do not look after themselves and nor do crops cultivate by themselves. Both require the daily attention of humans to prosper. For example, a typical day on a smallholding may involve some or all of the following: milking goats, feeding livestock, releasing poultry and fowl from their overnight housing, collecting eggs, removing animal droppings from stalls and sheds, freshening bedding, renewing water, leading goats and sheep to pasture, inspecting, watering and weeding crops, checking traps, a further round of milking, and securing chickens and ducks in houses before it gets dark.

With livestock quickly developing habits, a daily routine that can realistically be adhered to, which prioritizes and orders each task, should be planned and put into action. I have found that by having a comprehensive routine I go over each part of my holding every day and will therefore notice any changes to the animals' health, the integrity of the buildings and the presence of vermin and pests. A routine of daily chores ensures that the working smallholding remains tidy and, in addition, the presence of people milling around the place is a good way to deter pests, which are naturally wary of humans.

Buildings, in particular doorways, should be checked for signs of decay and repaired promptly.

ADEQUATE STORAGE FOR ANIMAL FEEDS AND MACHINERY

The majority of feed that the smallholder gives to his animals comes in 20–25kg bags, which are either bought as required, or in bulk of 1000kg and upwards from a local mill. In the case of the latter, a suitably secure structure of either wood, brick or galvanized metal will be required to safely store them where pests cannot get at them. When only a few bags at a time are used, they can be kept in purpose-built feed bins, which are pest-proof and most commonly kept in the building where the animal lives. Alternatively, they can be kept in dustbins placed in a large porch, or anywhere else that is easily accessible and vermin-proof. Bales of hay and straw will also need to be carefully stored, as they can be colonized rapidly by mice and rats. Bales can be stored inside, or outside with waterproof covering. I always take the precaution of stacking the bales in such a way so that I can walk around them; my terrier also has access to them so that he can flush out any pests. By being able to move around the bales I can place live capture traps in strategic positions and make regular inspections.

Logs and cut wood should be carefully stacked to avoid making a hiding place for pests.

These bales have been stacked in a way that is easy to inspect with gaps between them that my terrier can easily get through.

Essential items for keeping buildings and yards tidy.

Barns should never be used as a rubbish dump as pictured here.

Machinery, tools and equipment should be kept inside to protect them from the weather and so that they can be easily accessed and used. Many smallholders also have supplies of logs and wood for burning. These should never be left in random piles, which can often prove to be hideaways for rodents and sometimes even rabbits. All wood should be piled carefully, with no gaps or holes, in order to prevent this kind of harbourage.

UTILIZATION OF APPROPRIATE TOOLS AND EQUIPMENT

There is a vast range of equipment that can prove invaluable for the person endeavouring to keep his smallholding tidy. These range from tools for cleaning and sweeping up, to automatic livestock drinkers and feeders that prevent spilling. At the very least, the smallholder will need to invest in: a muck fork, shovel, yard brush, wheelbarrow and feed and water buckets for the variety of animals he keeps.

DISPOSAL OF RUBBISH AND BEDDING

Every advisory booklet concerning rodent control, produced by companies manufacturing rodenticides, warns against the practice of dumping rubbish, either in the corner of a building or on an out of the way bit of land, because of the living environment and cover they give to mice and rats. Rubbish must never be left to accumulate, but should be promptly disposed of, either by taking it to the council depot or incineration.

Animals that are kept inside will need to be regularly mucked out, which simply

Livestock barns will require regular mucking out.

involves the removal of soiled bedding material, most commonly straw or wood shavings. As this quite obviously cannot be taken to the council tip or burnt, the common and traditional solution is to make a muck heap. The intention is that the process of microbiological activity will break down the layers of waste into organic matter, which can then be used to enrich the land. The muck heap must be carefully sited so that it cannot leach into a water source of any description and is easy to access, irrespective of the weather conditions.

As well as soiled bedding from the goats and ponies, I add poultry droppings, vegetable peelings, weeds, grass and a small proportion of wood shavings to my heap. In time the size of the heap reduces, as carbon burns off and the bacteria living in the muck reproduce as it heats up, transforming the raw ingredients into valuable humus, which is considered a healing balm for the soil's wounds. The heat within the heap cooks the smell out of animal manure very effectively, so that it is not offensive to handle.

A suitable muck heap can be fashioned by Sir Albert Howard's 'Indore method', with the average pile being 2m wide, 60–150cm high and up to 10m long. Regular turning of the heap will promote aerobic activity and speed the rate of decomposition. An alternative approach to the heap can be utilized when the ground is to be left fallow for several months. In this situation, the organic waste material can be directly placed on the soil and raked out, until it is no deeper than 12cm, and left to decay. Once this has taken place, a rotivator can be used to work the organic matter into the soil, or chickens can be allowed to do the task due to their keenness for scratching at the soil. The chief advantage of this method is that none of the goodness is washed away through weathering, instead all the nutrients go directly into the soil.

My experience has taught me that it is best to keep the muck heap simple; avoid fencing it in for aesthetic reasons, or covering it to prevent it becoming waterlogged. Both these measures are likely to make the heap an inviting home for rodents and, additionally, can make it difficult to turn, particularly when machinery is being used. I remember the problems it caused when I carefully measured out a muck heap and put in posts, to which I attached corrugated metal sheets. Although this was a tidy way of marking the boundary of the land designated as the heap, the accumulation of straw next to the metal sheets made a safe haven for rats to hide away in. I did place some corrugated sheets on top of the straw waste to stop the rain getting at it; however, when I lifted the sheets after a week I found two large adult rats underneath it. Fortunately, I had my terrier with me and he scampered under the tin and within a few minutes killed them. Since then I have never covered or fenced in my muck heaps, choosing instead to rely on skill with the pitch fork to shape the heap so that it looks tidy, and is angled on the top so that the rain water can run off.

Having discussed the primary preventative measures of pest control, in the next chapter I shall look at the other tools that the smallholder can utilize.

A muck heap is best left uncovered to prevent pests from making it a home.

chapter four

The Pest Controller's Armoury

Go into any garden nursery or agricultural supplier and you will be confronted by what can be a bewildering array of pest control products, promising to deal effectively with everything from moles and rats, to crows and pigeons. Many of the products recently made available have been developed in response to demands for environmentally friendly and kinder, non-chemical alternatives to the more conventional products. There is certainly no shortage of choice and the novice may find himself unsure about which product to choose for a particular task. Fortunately, there is a certain amount of guidance to be gleaned from smallholder clubs and booklets produced by manufacturers; however, as with most things in life, first-hand experience is the most effective tutor.

The three things to consider when buying any pest control item are:

Ease of use

Consider how much time is required in the use of the selected method and whether any special skill or ability is needed.

Will it work?

There is no doubt that some techniques work better than others. The fact that some products have come and gone over the years while others have remained, emphasizes this point.

Will it continue to be effective over a prolonged period of time?

Some products can prove to be very effective at the outset, but over time animals may either lose their fear of them or develop immunity to their effects.

Bearing these points in mind I have built up an armoury over a couple of decades, which equips me to deal with the common pests and it consists of the following: various traps, rodenticide commonly referred to as poison, air rifles, dogs and ferrets, deterrents, repellents, electric fencing, bird scarers, automatic feeders, tree guards and crop protection in the form of polytunnels and horticultural netting. I shall now look briefly at the virtue of each of these, beginning with traps.

TRAPS

Traps are amongst the oldest tools used by man to catch animals and birds. The art of trapping is not as popular as it once was and has suffered from a tarnished reputation, owing to the widespread use of the gin or steel trap which, because it maimed so many animals, was unequivocally considered to be an instrument of torture. The development of poisons, which can be laid by professional and amateur pest controllers alike, also contributed to the demise of trapping. The situation today regarding the deployment of traps could not be in greater contrast to the period during the late nineteenth and early to mid-twentieth centuries, when the gin trap was commonly used by rabbit trappers and gamekeepers.

The new generation of lethal traps, known as spring traps, cannot be sold in Britain unless they have first been approved for use by the appropriate authority, such as DEFRA or the Scottish Executive. They scrutinize how humane the traps are in operation, by looking at how quickly they will kill the target animal and the actual mechanics of how this is achieved. In order to gain approval the trap has to kill instantly, using a powerful blow to the head or body of the intended victim. This ensures that no creature is subjected to unnecessary suffering; furthermore there are clear guidelines on how spring traps are to be set and on which animals they can be used, the rules in Britain are also stricter than those in North America and many parts of Europe. Therefore, the traps that are used in Britain today are well regulated and designed and, when set correctly, effective and quick acting. As a result the smallholder can rest assured that, in using traps, he is employing a humane pest control method.

I have a select collection of traps that I use regularly on my smallholding and some of these, such as the Fenn Mark IV spring trap and live capture traps, have multiple uses, but I will look first at traps which are permanently employed on the holding and these are mouse traps.

A typical, modern break-back mouse trap.

Mouse Traps

The mouse traps that I use are of the break-back variety and the multi-catch live trap. The break-back mouse trap is the traditional type that most members of the public will be familiar with. It dates from 1897 when Proctor Brothers released the 'Little Nipper', the original wooden platform mousetrap which, when set, was so sensitive to the movement of the mouse that it achieved a very high catch rate. Although the Little Nipper is still available it has, to some extent, been superseded by a new generation of break-back traps made primarily of plastic. The advantages of these are that they are easier to set, have a better baiting point and are more powerful than the wooden versions. They can also be emptied without the need to handle the dead mouse.

Whether made of wood, metal or plastic the mode of operation of all of these break-back traps is essentially the same. The bait is placed on a treadle or in a small station, which is often circular. As the sprung arm is pulled back and held in place, the treadle or platform is raised. Once the mouse steps on this platform the spring arm is released and hits the mouse with enough force to cause a quick death. The break-back traps have a proven record of success, are easy to deploy and result in a high number of catches. They will, however, require regular checking because constant usage may lead to faults occurring in the spring mechanism, which leads to either the trap going off prematurely, or the arm not being released when the mouse stands on the platform.

As its name suggests, the live multi-catch trap does not kill the mouse, but catches it alive. The scent of appropriate bait attracts the mouse into one of two entry tunnels and up an inclined plate, which acts like a seesaw. As the plate descends under the weight of the mouse, it raises a trap door, which prevents the creature exiting the same way it entered, and forces it to proceed into the main body of the trap. Once the mouse steps off the plate, it instantly returns to its inclined position so that the mouse is unable to escape. This means that the multi-catch trap is self-setting and can hold as many as ten mice, although the most that I have caught at one time is only four. With this trap measuring 15cm by 40cm, there is plenty of room for the mice to move about and, with a generous array of air vents, plenty of fresh air to ensure that the mice are not subjected to unnecessary discomfort.

The multi-catch is the only type of live trap for mice that I like to use because I do not feel that the smaller, single-catch versions provide the features mentioned and, as a result, are unpleasant for the mice and can lead to overheating. When using the multi-catch live trap, the smallholder must assume responsibility for checking it at least twice a day and either humanely dispatching, or releasing what is caught. Having a trap that can catch up to ten mice at once is a great advantage when there

Multi-catch mouse trap with see-through lid for easy inspection. STV INTERNATIONAL

is a dense resident population of the little pest. The trap can easily be placed under pallets on which bags of livestock feed are stacked, or where livestock are present, without them being able to interfere with the operation of the trap, which would be the case if a break-back trap was used. The only maintenance this trap requires is routine cleaning; this involves checking that no bait has been taken under the inclined plates, which appears to be the favourite place for the caught mice to hide. If the bait is of a cereal type and grains get lodged under the plates, it stops them returning fully to their inclined positions and offers the mice a chance to escape.

Spring Traps

Although more powerful break-back traps are marketed for catching rats, I prefer to use larger spring traps for this purpose. This is because the forceful 125mm jaws are big enough to grip both the head and body of a rat and deliver a quick, lethal blow. The spring traps that are available in Britain today are the product of work undertaken by the Humane Traps Advisory Committee established in 1954, the National Institute of Agricultural Engineering and individual

A couple of Fenn spring traps.

I use the Fenn Mark IV primarily on rats and it has proved to be consistently effective. Although it is not a difficult trap to set, two hands will be needed to open the jaws until they are level with the plate. In this position a safety hook is swung over one of the jaws, to ensure safe handling of the trap while the trapper puts it in place.

Generally a number of Fenn traps will need to be used in conjunction to ensure success, but they are inexpensive (currently retailing for somewhere around £10). Attention also has to be paid to placing the trap in the correct location, at the right level within the tunnel and on a fine enough setting to ensure success. There are other similar spring traps available in Britain, which do the same job as the Fenn Mark IV: among these are the Sawyer, Solway and Juby traps.

LIVE TRAPS

trap designers and were developed to fill the gap left by cruel, steel leg hold traps, which were outlawed in 1957 in England and Wales and in 1973 in Scotland.

The spring trap that I use most often is known as a Fenn Mark IV trap, which is one of the oldest British spring traps. It is named after its inventor, Arthur Fenn from Worcestershire and has become the most commonly used trap of its type in this country. The trap may legally be used to kill: rats, grey squirrels, weasels and stoats. However, they must be set in protective tunnels in order to prevent animals, other than the target species, whether domestic or wild, getting injured by the trap. In terms of achieving what are referred to as quick or humane kills, extensive studies have confirmed that the Fenn trap has a 90 per cent success rate and the minority of failures were attributed to faulty setting.

There are an assortment of these traps, which vary in size, depending upon which animal they are to be used on. There are live traps available for catching: rats, grey squirrels, weasels and stoats, mink, rabbits and foxes. They are constructed of weld mesh wire and all work in essentially the same manner. Appropriate bait is used to entice the target animal into the trap, which is generally rectangular in shape. In order to get the bait the animal has to stand on a slightly inclined treadle, which, under the pressure of the weight, releases a retaining hook, which, in turn, instantly closes the trap door.

Although they are easy traps to set, the real skill is knowing the best place to put them and the trapper has to possess the patience to let them remain in the same place – sometimes for as long as a week – before he catches anything. The smallholder who chooses to use these

A variety of live capture traps suitable for small mammals, ranging from a weasel to a rabbit.

kinds of traps will have to promptly and humanely dispatch whatever is caught. For this reason, and because I feel there are easier ways to deal with foxes, I do not use a live capture fox trap, preferring instead to limit my activities to the smaller mammals. The great advantage of live capture traps is that they cannot harm animals and so are perfectly safe to use where poultry and livestock are kept. An indicator of how popular these types of traps have become is reflected in the statistics of one leading company, which recorded sales exceeding 50,000 for two years in a row.

CLAW TRAP

This trap is known by various names including: claw, pincer, tongs and scissors. It is a spring-operated trap, though markedly different in shape from the spring traps previously discussed and this highlights the fact that it is a specialized trap with just one purpose, which is to catch the subterranean mole. The trap has two powerful jaws which, when triggered, clamp around the mole's body causing a quick death. As the arms, also known as bars, are left protruding above the ground it is easy to identify if the trap has been activated by assessing the width between the arms. In the set position the arms are just 70mm apart,

Claw or scissors trap for catching moles.
STV INTERNATIONAL

whereas when they have been released, the distance is 120mm. This trap has, for a long time, been the first choice of the traditional mole catcher and continues to be one of the surest ways of controlling the animal. Although a number of these traps may be required to achieve success, the most crucial factor is the correct siting of them in the mole's tunnels.

RODENTICIDES

It was not until after the Second World War that poison became widely used, in efforts to control rats and mice. The initial poison was the well-known anti-coagulant warfarin, which inhibits the role of vitamin K in the process of clotting and, in excessive doses, causes death by haemorrhaging of the internal organs. The poisons that are listed as rodenticides and commonly used

71

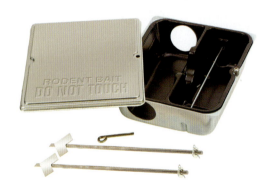

A top quality bait station to be used in conjunction with poison. STV INTERNATIONAL

today are known as 'second generation anti-coagulants' and include difenacoum and bromadioline. The poisons available to the amateur pest controller will have difenacoum as the active ingredient and this is an estimated 100 times more powerful than warfarin, which means that it will kill the rat or mouse quicker, with less of the poison having to be consumed in order to achieve this. To some extent this reduces the animal's suffering, however, their strength has raised concerns that other animals, in particular birds of prey, are susceptible to the phenomenon known as 'secondary poisoning'. This occurs when they eat rats or mice that have died as a result of consuming rodenticide; it has been claimed that the eating of just two poisoned mice is sufficient to kill an owl. Consequently the smallholder must assume responsibility for correctly disposing of any poisoned rodents.

While rodenticides are inherently dangerous substances, a great deal can be done to ensure that they are not hazardous to humans or non-target animals, such as the dogs and livestock typically found on a smallholding. They should always be stored in a secure place and used only in conjunction with one of the vast array of bait stations. A red or blue dye is also commonly added to rodenticides so that the user is able to easily identify any spillage. In order to make the poison palatable the anti-coagulant is mixed with whole or cut wheat, depending on whether it is intended for rats or mice. Modern poisons are available in various forms, ranging from the typical granules to paraffin wax blocks, which are capable of remaining fresh and palatable, even in wet conditions.

The use of poison is a simple control method that anybody can master and it has the added benefits of not consuming a great deal of time and being consistently effective. However, rats in particular can be incredibly suspicious of anything new or unfamiliar in their environment and, consequently, are sometimes slower than expected to take the poison. Since I have an ongoing pest control programme, I only encounter rats occasionally and then in small numbers. As a result I use poison as a last line of defence if the traps, shooting, or a terrier are unable to deal with the intruders. However, there is no doubt that those subjected to a substantial rodent infestation will, within a seven to ten-day period, experience a dramatic reduction in their numbers if an assortment of primed bait stations are placed in strategic positions.

AIR RIFLE

The air rifle is a well-known and recognized tool of the traditional pest controller. It has been employed with great success to deal with major infestations of: rats, grey squirrels, crows and pigeons, albeit mostly by airgun enthusiasts or professionals, who are willing to spend many hours at a time using their rifles. Even though the majority of smallholders may not wish to invest this amount of time pursuing pests with an air rifle, there is still a great deal that can be achieved with it, as I have observed on my smallholding. Here my brother, who has written two books on the use of air rifles and is a regular contributor to the *Airgunner* magazine, always keeps a rifle nearby when he is working around the barns or in the vegetable plot, so that he is able to take the opportunities to shoot pests as they arise. This takes him very little time and yet has proved to be one of the most effective ways to maintain pests at a manageable level.

The air rifle can be used by the pest controller in two ways:

1. As a primary tool for shooting pests at distances of 10–40m.
2. As a secondary tool for shooting pests that have first been trapped. This is done at what is referred to as 'point blank range', which many people, understandably, find unpleasant.

An air rifle is suitable for shooting many of the pests that appear on the smallholding.

Having limited power, due to British legislation and the design of the weapon, the air rifle is only suitable for killing pests at a distance not exceeding 40m. This is only a fraction of the distance a firearm certificated bullet rifle is capable of firing. However, unlike firearms, the air rifle can safely be used within barns and outbuildings, which is where a great deal of the smallholder's pest control is required. Added to this, the discharge of an air rifle with a silencer, which is now considered a common feature, does not scare livestock. I observed this when my chickens, displaying insatiable curiosity and little concern for their safety, strolled onto my brother's practice range when he was shooting at targets.

The modern phenomenon of the pre-charged pneumatic (PCP) air rifle makes accurate shooting a relatively easy skill to master, due to the absence of recoil, commonly encountered when using traditional spring air rifles. However, the air rifle user also has to be fully conversant with how scopes and pellets work and have the know-how to approach the pests, without scaring them away before he can take a shot. Success will also depend on his ability to judge distance, compensate for any effect the weather may have on the flight of the pellet and the selection of a suitable shooting position.

The air rifle may be legally employed to shoot the following pests:

- Birds: crows, rooks, jackdaws, magpies, jays, wood pigeon, feral pigeon and collared doves.
- Mammals: brown rats, grey squirrels, stoats, weasels, mink and rabbits.

It must always be borne in mind that the smallholder who chooses to utilize an air rifle, automatically assumes a legal and ethical responsibility to use it in a safe and humane fashion.

DOGS AND FERRETS

A dog was a familiar sight accompanying the cottagers, crofters and farmers of bygone times. Although they were company for men who would spend a lot of time alone, the dog would often perform a number of vital tasks, including the protection of livestock and control of vermin. They realized that the presence of a dog would ward off foxes from vulnerable livestock and that their hunting instinct would compel them to pursue rabbits and rats with equal enthusiasm. Some breeds, such as the terriers, earned a reputation as specialist vermin controllers; however, in more recent times, the widespread ownership of firearms and use of poisons have tended to eclipse the traditional role of the dog in this respect.

Nevertheless, the dog can continue to play an important part in keeping the modern smallholding free from pests. Although some breeds are better at this kind of work than others, there are very few dogs that have nothing to offer. In fact, a great deal depends on the owner's understanding of how to direct his dog to do this type of work. There is no doubt that, as a result of keeping dogs purely as companions, they are often an overlooked resource, as many people are not familiar with how to train or use their dogs to control pests.

The mere sight or sound of a dog on a smallholding has been sufficient to scare away foxes and deer, and most dogs will enthusiastically hunt the smaller pests if they are given the opportunity. For example, the late countryman Phil Drabble used his pointer, Tick, and Alsatian, Belle, both

The terrier and ferret are a traditional combination for dealing with rats and rabbits.

breeds that are not commonly associated with rodent control, to kill seventy rats around his yard and buildings during one year. Another example is provided by the exploits of the canine expert Brian Plummer, who trained a Cavalier King Charles spaniel (which belongs to the toy dog group) to catch rabbits.

With their acute senses of smell and hearing, dogs also have the ability to detect the presence of pests living in the outbuildings or passing through the fields, long before a person will notice. This is an invaluable service because it enables the smallholder to deal with pests before they have a chance to establish themselves or cause much damage. However, an ability to read the expression of the dog by the handler is essential in order to achieve this and it takes time to acquire this skill, as it does to train the dog for the task of pest control. One professional claimed that it might take as long as five years before the dog and owner truly become an expert partnership.

Another animal that has a lot to offer the smallholder who wants to control pests is the ferret. The domestic ferret has been used in Britain for approximately 800 years to catch rabbits and is still considered one of the most effective ways of doing so. Basically the ferret is used to drive rabbits from their warrens into pre-set nets, which entangle the creatures as they bolt into them. In this way a substantial number of rabbits can be caught during the course of one day. Although it is a straightforward process, ferreting can be time consuming and exhausting work; it is also a seasonal activity, taking place during the cold weather of late autumn and winter.

The advantage of using ferrets in this way is that, in addition to controlling one of the most troublesome of pests to those growing crops and vegetables, it is also an ideal way to acquire a free supply of healthy meat. For those who are creative, the skins or pelts can also be cured and made into garments to keep the smallholder warm in winter. Consequently, for those people who are pursuing smallholding in an effort to be self-sufficient, the wild rabbit is a valuable resource.

Ferrets make fierce hunters and they hate rats. This enmity means that they can also be used to either flush rats from their hiding places into the path of a waiting dog, or kill them where they are hiding. The rat can be a savage fighter, but its natural impulse is to flee from a ferret. Nevertheless, a ferret should never be expected to deal with a major rat infestation single-handed. I will only pit my ferret against a single rat, generally when it has been cornered and has nowhere to run; in all such situations the ferret has quickly killed the rat without being injured in any way.

If opting to keep ferrets, the smallholder will have to be prepared to clean their cages, feed and exercise them every day. This does not require a lot of time and the ferrets can be fed on parts of the rabbit that are not used in cooking. The ferret must be kept in a secure cage or shed, because they will quickly wreak havoc if they gain

Ferrets need to be kept in a secure well-ventilated cage.

their freedom and encounter poultry and fowl. Although they can be playful and entertaining animals to keep, it is clear that ferrets are not worth the pest controller bothering with if there is a scarcity of rabbits in the area he lives in.

DETERRENTS/REPELLENTS

There are a growing number of smallholders who do not wish to use lethal means of control on any pests, other than the rodents, and as a result the modern range of deterrents and repellents are fast becoming their primary tools for this task.

Although the deterrents generally cover a relatively small area, extending from approximately 8–15m in an arc of 110 degrees, careful positioning, or the employment of a number of such devices, can compensate for this. They have been made waterproof so that they are suitable for outside applications and are easy to install and portable because they are battery powered. There are a few models that can also be run off mains electricity, however, the average smallholding is unlikely to have an appropriate socket near to some of the areas where the deterrent will be required. Unfortunately, the deterrent I have tested is not recommended for use with rechargeable batteries, but battery life can be extended by adjusting the settings for the volume and length of time the deterrent remains on: typical battery life when in daily use is 100 hours.

The deterrents use light, sound or water to scare an animal into taking flight and are activated by the animal triggering a passive, infra-red (PIR) motion detector. Once the deterrent is activated it can remain on for between fifteen seconds and seven minutes, depending on the setting selected. Deterrents are primarily aimed at scaring deer and foxes and are probably

Wildlife deterrent that uses light and sound to scare pests into fleeing. STV INTERNATIONAL

more effective in rural areas, where animals continue to exhibit their instinctive wariness, compared to more urban areas where even flighty deer are growing accustomed to the panoply of noises made by humans. There is the possibility of deterrents being triggered by branches of nearby trees blowing in the wind, or animals other than those for which it was intended. It is also possible that, should it remain in the same position for a prolonged period of time, there is a chance that the target animals, in particular foxes, will grow accustomed to the noise, shining light or jet of water the deterrent emits and consequently ignore it.

Animal repellents utilize a substance that the targeted pests so dislike the taste or smell of, they will vacate the area without causing any actual damage. The active ingredient in most of these products comes from a natural, as opposed to a chemical, source and is so species-specific that only

Repellents are available for dealing with moles, rabbits and squirrels.

the targeted pests finds it repugnant. Consequently, they are incapable of harming livestock or children and have been developed to deal with the unwanted attentions of grey squirrels and moles, in the form of a liquid spray and granules respectively. There is also a repellent aimed at deterring rabbits and other wild animals, such as deer and foxes, from causing damage. In this case the active ingredient is aluminium ammonium sulphate in powder form which, when it is made into a liquid, can be sprayed directly onto vegetables without doing them any harm.

Repellents will have to be applied repeatedly in order to offer ongoing protection and only cover a limited area of ground; typically the size of a garden, as opposed to the many acres of a smallholding, as it would be an expensive endeavour to employ repellents on such a large scale. Nevertheless, repellents can prove to be beneficial when the smallholder wishes to safeguard the growth of young vegetable plants, which are so easily devastated by munching rabbits and undermined by tunnelling moles. There is also a risk that a repellent will simply make the targeted animal concentrate its attention on another part of the smallholding, until the effect has worn off on the treated ground. In addition rain may have a detrimental effect on some repellents, necessitating re-application following wet weather. For these reasons I never rely purely on repellents, but use them in conjunction with other pest control tools.

ELECTRIC FENCING

An effective strategy for both preventing pests damaging growing crops and protecting vulnerable livestock, such as poultry and new-born lambs, from predatory pests is to place a protective barrier around them; one of the most popular ways of doing this is to use electric fencing. Unlike other barriers which are, in effect, obstacles that are too difficult for pests to clamber over or jump, the electric fence works by delivering a momentary painful shock to any animal that touches it, prompting it, at the very least, to halt in its tracks and more commonly to flee.

For those who have watched spy and war films, electric fencing may conjure up images of high fencing enclosing military

This poultry netting deters pests by giving them an electric shock when they touch it.

touching the fence an animal completes the circuit, resulting in a momentary shock and the electrical pulse travels back through the ground to the energizer. This is only possible because of the earth stake, which incorporates the ground into the system.

There are an assortment of optional additional items available, which make it easier to set up and move the fence and increase its efficiency. These include: reels, insulators, gate handles, tensioners, cut-off switches and fault finders.

The use of electric fencing in Britain dates back nearly fifty years; it is a very popular tool of the smallholder because it is easy to install and requires a minimal amount of maintenance, as well as being both affordable and reliable. The most common problems encountered with electric fencing are attributed to incorrect earthing, or draining of the electrical charge, due to long grass touching the bottom strands of the fencing. Both of these are human errors, which can be easily avoided. Although electric fencing provides the smallholder with peace of mind that his livestock and crops have adequate protection, he will have to take adequate precautions to prevent children or pets coming into contact with an energized fence.

establishments and delivering agonizing, near lethal shocks to anyone foolish enough to touch them. Such images are in stark contrast to the modern electric fencing, intended for agricultural and smallholding purposes. This has been developed with input from universities and DEFRA and subjected to European safety initiatives, which ensure that the shock does not reach a harmful level, even if a person or animal inadvertently gets trapped on the fence.

Essentially an electric fence consists of the following components:

- An energizer that provides the fence with its electrical pulse or charge.
- Either plastic, metal or wooden posts.
- Either polyurethane netting, poly-tape or poly-wire, which all conduct the electrical charge, due to metal filaments contained within their strands.
- An earth stake. The electric fence is an open circuit, consisting of the fence itself and the ground on which it stands. On

BIRD SCARERS

The primary purpose of bird scarers is to prevent birds stealing seed or damaging crops and they have been in use, in one form or another, for as long as men have tilled the ground. Farm workers during the late eighteenth century would routinely take a break from working their heavy horses to shoot at starlings and crows with catapults; as recently as the early twentieth century, boys would be employed to walk around fields with wooden clappers to scare birds away. There is an assortment of bird scarers available today which utilize noise, movement or reflected light to scare birds. The most common one used by farmers is the gas-powered bird scarer, which generates an intermittent explosive noise, similar to the report of a rifle. Some countrymen, such as the late Phil Drabble, have questioned the effectiveness of these devices, observing that birds often return to the crops in between the bangs and wildlife quickly becomes acquainted with the noise and learns that it actually does them no harm.

In an effort to tackle birds traditional scarecrows were made by enterprising people in bygone days, with the intention of mimicking the presence of a person in a field; however, the stationary nature of these objects rendered them ineffective. Armed with this knowledge, contemporary designers have fashioned bird scarers that rectify this fault by moving continuously in a rotary action. They also generally incorporate a large reflective strip, featuring the eyes of a predator to further deter birds. Lines of repeller tape operate in a similar way, as its holographic flashes rays of reflected sunlight, complemented in light winds with a metallic rattling noise.

Gardeners often make their own bird scarers, commonly using the shining surfaces of unwanted CDs and DVDs, hanging them from string so that they move in the breeze. Whether bought or home-made, the combination of light and movement that these scarers utilize is a simple and proven deterrent. However, their continued effectiveness depends to a great extent on their position being changed routinely, in order to prevent birds becoming accustomed to them and ignoring them.

Modern bird scarer with rotating reflective head.
STV INTERNATIONAL

AUTOMATIC POULTRY FEEDERS

Wild birds, grey squirrels and rodents all possess an appetite for the feed that the smallholder gives to his poultry and fowl. This can lead to both contamination and substantial waste of feed and, as a consequence, drive up the cost of home egg production. One way of preventing this is to kill the pests. Another is to deny them

Home-made scarecrow.

access to the costly feed in the first place and this is achieved by employing automatic feeders, such as the 'Grandpa's Chicken Feeder', developed in New Zealand over fifteen years ago and now commonly used in Britain.

They feature a lid over the feed, which is pivoted open by the weight of the chicken as it stands on a platform. Once the chicken has completed feeding and steps off the platform, the lid closes so that there is no way for wild animals to get at the valuable contents. Being constructed of galvanized metal they cannot be gnawed or pecked through and keep the feed dry and fresh so that it remains palatable. They also have the advantage of only needing filling once or twice a week, depending on the number of birds being kept. When using an automatic feeder, the smallholder has to take the time to introduce his chickens to it slowly and should never leave the lid in the closed position, until he is absolutely sure that his birds know how to use it and are happy to operate the feeder independently; some breeds of chicken may take longer than others to get used to it.

TREE GUARDS

Healthy woodlands and orchards can make a considerable contribution to the smallholder becoming self-sufficient, by providing wood for fuel and building projects and food in the form of fruits and nuts. In addition, trees can be grown to form vital windbreaks and the prunings of some species are used as a complementary feed for livestock. Whatever the case, trees need looking after, particularly in the early years of growth when they are most likely to be eaten or damaged. The most obvious way to protect them is to stop an animal, whether it is a lowly rabbit or a regal deer, getting at the trees by placing a guard around them. These are rectangular or cylindrical in shape and typically about 100cm high. In this way a newly planted sapling is entirely enclosed until it has rooted and grown to a certain height, which often takes a couple of years.

On more established trees, larger guards are used to cover the most vulnerable part of the trunk so that it cannot be debarked. These guards take little time or effort to put in place and ensure that the tree can grow without setbacks. They can be purchased ready for use or made at home, should alternate dimensions to the standard bought ones be required. I have known people who have gone to great lengths to prepare the ground for saplings, plant them carefully and water and feed them diligently, only to see all their hard work go to waste simply because they omitted to place any form of guard around the trees. Consequently, there was nothing

Automatic poultry feeder prevents pellets being stolen.

Tree guards are an easy and effective way to protect saplings.

to stop the rabbits stripping the bark for food during the first bout of prolonged bad winter weather.

CROP PROTECTION

In the same way as poultry feed and trees are safeguarded by taking measures to prevent pests getting at them, vegetable and fruit crops can also be protected from the destructive habits of pests by placing structures over them, which deprive animals of any opportunity to come into contact with the valuable crops.

Polytunnels are a common sight in large vegetable gardens and on smallholdings because they extend the growing season, resulting in an increased harvest. In addition to providing a temperate environment for optimum growing, a polytunnel prevents damage being caused to fruit and vegetables by denying pests access. These dome-shaped structures have premium-grade polythene, stretched taut over thick galvanized metal bars and buried in the ground to hold them secure, which proves an effective barrier to burrowing rabbits. The only pests that I have known to get into a polytunnel are mice and they can easily be lured into live traps, kept in the polytunnel throughout the growing season. Polytunnels do, however, have their limitations. Unless setting up on a commercial scale, they do not have the space needed for large crops and are clearly more suited to fruit and vegetables, which flourish in hot conditions; even then well planned irrigation is required.

It cannot be denied that the bulk of vegetables, which typically constitute the staple portion of the British diet, grow best

As well as extending the growing season, cloches offer vegetables protection.

outside. Recognizing this, some firms now offer structures resembling a polytunnel in shape, but with netting instead of polythene stretched over heavy duty PVC tubes. This has the benefit of exposing the vegetables to the weather while still keeping pests, such as wild birds and rabbits, out. They are made to a sufficient height to allow a person easy access, so that he is able to inspect and weed the crop. A less expensive alternative can be fashioned by simply stretching horticultural netting over the vegetables requiring protection and holding it in place with stakes. This is probably the best option when there are large areas to be covered.

Ripening fruit is particularly susceptible to attack by birds, which have the annoying habit of stealing the fruit before the grower gets the opportunity to pick it. The common solution to this is to use a fruit cage, which is constructed of galvanized metal pipes and covered with strong nylon netting. Such cages are generally high enough for a person to walk underneath and are easily added on to should the need arise. Although the initial cost of a fruit cage can be considerable, once it is in position it will offer effortless and effective protection from pests for many years. They are quite simple structures and can be made using wood that is 48mm by 48mm thick for the frame and standard horticultural netting as a cover. In the following chapters I shall describe in detail the practical steps that must be taken when employing the tools mentioned in this chapter.

chapter five

How to Use Traps

Anyone who wants to make use of traps should bear in mind that he will be responsible for ensuring that:

- Only approved traps are employed.
- They are used solely for their intended purpose.
- They do not present a danger to non-target species, livestock, children or adults.
- The traps are checked on a regular basis, so that what is caught or killed may be dealt with appropriately.
- When necessary, animals that are caught in live traps are killed in a humane manner.

Although it takes time and experience to acquire the skills of an accomplished trapper, the novice will be able to achieve success if he abides by the following basic rules:

- Use a proven bait that is appealing to the target animal.
- Select the best location for the trap, which should be within the target animal's territory and, where possible, on the paths it travels from its hideaway to its intended food source.
- Always double-check that the process of setting the trap has been correctly carried out.

I shall now show how each of these basic rules can be applied to the variety of traps

that I use on my smallholding, to keep the outbuildings and land free from pests.

THE BREAK-BACK MOUSETRAP

Thanks to modern innovations, this traditional type of mouse trap is both safe and easy to use.

Bait

All of the various versions of break-back mouse traps require appropriate bait. Cheese has been the common choice for many decades and has proved reasonably successful. The stronger cheeses, such as Stilton and mature cheddar, have a pungent smell that seems particularly alluring to mice. A great variety of other baits have also been used including: chocolate, dried fruit, peanut butter and pieces of cake, or whatever else is leftover in the kitchen. Nowadays specially formulated baits are also available, ready for use in syringes to enable simple dispensing.

It is worth bearing in mind that mice, in particular house mice, will eat nearly anything and, in the case of the break-back trap, the consistency of the bait is of primary concern. In the early days when these traps had spoon- or fork-like bait holders, the bait had to be reasonably solid so that it could be either tied or pushed on, otherwise the mouse could sometimes snatch the

Bait reservoirs on break-back mouse trap with the left one filled.

bait away without actually triggering the trap. Today's traps feature much better bait reservoirs, or stations actually built on the base of the trap. Consequently, there is no longer the need to use solid bait and I always select something that can be pressed firmly into the station, such as tiny bits of soft bread covered with jam, so that it is difficult for the mouse to move and necessitates it standing on the weight-sensitive platform. Irrespective of what bait is selected, it should be changed every five to seven days because exposure to air dries it out and makes it less palatable. The bait should always be placed in the trap when it is closed and therefore cannot snap shut on the fingers.

Siting and Setting the Trap

With the trap baited it can be taken to the required location. This will be where copious amounts of droppings, gnawing of wood and damage to feed sacks, will have betrayed the presence of mice. Although careful concealment of the trap is not necessary, wherever possible it should be placed next to a wall or other such feature that the mice are likely to travel along. When there is the possibility of the trap being set off by anything other than mice, it can be placed in a bought or home-made trap box. With the trap in position it is set by simply pulling back the trigger arm until it clicks into place. The trap should be checked every day, preferably in the morning, as mice are most likely to be caught during the night. It is a feature of modern traps that dead mice can be removed without actually having to touch them, just by raising the trigger arm. If a dead mouse is left in the trap for several days, the pressure of the arm on the skull digs into the flesh and the mouse gets stuck to the trap and has to be pulled off. I dispose of dead mice by feeding them to my ferrets, as I am aware that they are fresh and have not been killed by poison. Alternatively, it is an acceptable practice to bury small numbers of mice.

A break-back trap with catch.

MULTI-CATCH MOUSE TRAP

Bait

A different type of bait from that used with break-back traps, is preferred for the multi-catch mouse trap. This is simply because the mouse is caught in the process of travelling down the trap's tunnel on its way to the luring bait, as opposed to being trapped while trying to steal the bait. Solid grains such as: barley, oats, maize or flaked peas are ideal; they also stay fresher for a longer period of time than other types of bait, which is an advantage because the multi-catch, unlike the break-back trap, is suitable for constant use as a preventative measure. Furthermore, this bait is the type of food that mice are most likely to search for when entering an outbuilding and it is sufficiently enticing to tempt them into the trap. To bait the trap you simply raise the lid and place the grain inside and then close the lid. I always put a generous sprinkling of grain inside so that there is plenty for the mice to eat, in the event of more than one being caught.

Siting and Setting the Trap

This trap should be placed in the same location in barns and outbuildings as the break-back trap. In addition, as already mentioned, it can be used in areas which mice are likely to try to target but, at the time of setting, have not colonized, such as feed stores. With its low profile, the trap is ideal for these situations because it is easily pushed under the pallets on which feed

The mouse has plenty of room to move about, which stops it getting distressed or overheating.

Grain bait placed in a multi-catch mouse trap.

A field mouse being released where it will do no harm.

sacks are typically stacked. The multi-catch trap should be inspected each morning and the inclusion of a see-through panel in the lid makes this an easy task. Any mice that are caught should be promptly dealt with and the two options are either to release them or kill them. In the latter case this must be done humanely – dropping the trap in a bucket of water to drown the mice is no longer considered acceptable. Instead it is recommended that the mice be emptied into a sack and then hit quickly, with sufficient force, using a weighted stick.

FENN MARK IV

This is one of the most useful kill traps that the smallholder can employ because it is suitable for controlling: rats, weasels, stoats and grey squirrels. Despite this, I only use the trap to catch rats and it is in this respect that I shall describe its use, as I prefer to adopt alternative techniques for the other mammals mentioned. The fact that the Fenn trap does not require any bait, highlights how important it is to site and set the trap correctly.

Siting and Setting the Trap

The first task, even before picking up the trap, is to search for the tell-tale signs of rats such as: droppings, greasy smears and gnawing damage, as they will provide indicators of the path that the rat is travelling along and, consequently, a suitable place for setting the Fenn trap. Such paths are most commonly situated near a feature like a wall or straw bales, because they give the rodent, which feels vulnerable in open ground, a sense of security. Note should be taken of the most probable port of entry into the building and where the greatest degree of damage and amount of droppings are to be found. At these points,

tunnels measuring approximately 40cm long and 15cm high and wide should be placed. This is in order to comply with the guidelines for the safe deployment of the Fenn trap, which stipulate that the set trap should always be placed within a tunnel. These can be cobbled together with bricks that are lying about, made of wood, or a drain pipe with a diameter of 15cm may be used. Irrespective of which type of tunnel is employed, every effort should be made to make it blend in with the surrounding environment, so that it does not appear strange and arouse the suspicion of the cautious rat.

The process of setting the Fenn trap is quite straightforward and is as follows:

1. With the trap held in both hands, rest all the fingers of both hands on the underside of the trap. Insert the left thumb through the ring on the left jaw of the trap and place the right thumb on the corresponding right jaw. Apply pressure with the thumbs and pull the opposing jaws downwards, until they are level with the treadle plate. Move the right forefinger to the safety hook, while keeping all the other fingers underneath the trap. Rotate the safety hook with this finger so that it clamps over the right jaw of the trap.

2. Taking care not to disengage the safety hook, the brass plate is flipped forward with the right forefinger so that it covers the jaw. At the same time the treadle plate is pushed upwards with the fingers of the left hand, which are resting under the bottom of the trap. This enables the brass plate to be slotted into the corresponding catch on the treadle plate. The lightness of the trap setting is adjusted by the amount of the brass plate that is placed under the catch. To place the trap on its most sensitive setting, slide

Setting a Fenn trap. With the fingers under the base plate the thumbs are used to pull the jaws of the trap apart.

Engaging the safety hook.

merely 1–2mm of the brass plate under the catch.

3. The Fenn trap is now ready to be placed within a suitable tunnel. In the case of the drain tunnel the trap, still with the safety catch engaged, is pushed into the midsection, where a liberal amount of either leaves, straw or even floor sweepings are sprinkled over it. Finally, the safety hook is disengaged using a piece of strong wire with a bent end. Alternatively, when using a box tunnel the trap is placed on the floor where it is required, covered with a suitable material to conceal its outline, the safety hook is removed and then the tunnel carefully placed over the trap.

The trap should be inspected every morning, even if nothing has been caught; on no account should it be hastily moved, because it can take as long as a week for a rat to relax its suspicions sufficiently to be willing to travel through the tunnel and on to the trap. When a rat is found in the trap, the first thing to do is to check that it is dead, which it should be if the trap has been set correctly. However, in the event that a rat is caught in the trap and found to be still alive it must be killed instantly. Countrymen like my late grandfather, faced with such a situation, would have grabbed the nearest spade and dealt the rat a hefty blow, but this runs the risk of damaging the trap and may not always succeed in rapidly killing the rodent. I prefer to use an air rifle because it is a more controlled and precise method.

The brass plate being slid under the catch on the treadle plate.

A set spring trap must always be placed in a tunnel.

Fenn trap with catch showing how it fastens round the rat's body.

To release a dead rat, the trap is turned upside down and the jaws pulled slightly open so that the rat falls out of the trap, after which it should be disposed of by burying. The best practice for handling dead rats is to wear a pair of rubber gloves, which are used solely for this purpose; however, even if a dead rat is inadvertently touched with ungloved hands, provided they are washed thoroughly immediately afterwards there is no real danger of infection.

If the smallholder wishes to use the Fenn trap to catch weasels, stoats or grey squirrels, the process for setting the trap is undertaken in exactly the same way. The same rule of siting the trap along the course of the path that the particular animal routinely travels along still applies. In the case of these animals, such paths will typically be located near the base of hedges or in the bottom of ditches.

CLAW TRAP

The claw or scissors trap, designed for catching moles, is like the Fenn trap in the respect that it is not baited and the true skill is in the placing of them.

Setting and Siting

Where there is a cluster or abundance of mole hills, identify those that have fresh deposits of soil pushed up. The next step is to ascertain exactly where and at what depths the mole tunnels are located. This is achieved by using either a metal probe or sharpened hardwood stick, suitable for pushing into the ground. Some mole catchers prod the ground that lies between two mole hills, while others concentrate on the centre of the mole hill itself after pushing aside the fresh excavation of soil. In my experience, it is much easier to find the tunnel when the latter approach is employed. In either case, the probe is pushed into the ground until it meets no resistance, which indicates the finding of a mole tunnel.

Tunnels may be found at varying depths and the deeper ones, which are approximately 10–15cm below the surface, are more likely to be used by the mole

A selection of mole-catching equipment.

than shallow tunnels. When a tunnel is identified, a small trowel is used to excavate a hole large enough to insert the trap into. After removing a square of turf measuring 15cm by 20cm, the soil is carefully removed until the depth of the tunnel is reached, which should be free from the presence of rootlets and worm casts, because these are signs of disuse. Some trappers favour moulding loose soil onto the ring of the trigger mechanism in order to conceal the metal outline of the trap.

With one hand close the pincer-like ends together, so that the jaws of the trap are opened. Position the ring in the centre of the open jaws, so that the notches cut out of the top of the metal tongue slot into the left and right bars respectively. Not only does the tongue hold the jaws open in the set position, it also acts as a trigger, which releases the jaws to crush the mole when it pushes against the ring. With the trap set, it is placed in the prepared hole so that the ring is in line with the tunnel.

Using a probe to gauge depth of mole tunnel, before scraping the raised soil out of the way.

Mole tunnel uncovered.

Scissors trap in set position.

RIGHT: Trap placed in the hole, with the ring in line with the tunnel.

The open arms of the scissors trap above ground indicate a catch.

Scissors trap with catch.

There are two schools of thought regarding the filling in of the hole. Most commonly it is carefully filled around the trap, with the turf repositioned around the protruding arms so that, in essence, it is sealed. Others suggest leaving a slight gap around the trap so that a draught is created, which the mole will travel along the tunnel to block and in the process engage the trap. The trap should be checked every morning, which is straightforward as the protruding arms indicate when something is caught. It used to be that mole skins were sold to furriers but, unless the smallholder has an interest in treating skins, the mole is best disposed of by burying in the hole that the trap has been removed from, or fed to ferrets.

LIVE TRAPS

Rat Cage Trap

Although this trap was designed for catching rats, it can also be used to trap: grey squirrels, weasels, stoats and stray ferrets, providing that appropriate bait is placed in the trap. When selecting bait, think about the target animal's natural diet, as well as the type of food that is attracting it onto your smallholding. I have enjoyed success with the following:

- For rats: whole grains mixed with a small amount of molasses or treacle.
- For grey squirrels: any type of fruit, including citrus and bananas, nuts and maize.
- For weasels, stoats and ferrets: rabbit offal, raw eggs or the wing of a bird.

As in the case of the spring trap, the cage trap should be placed where there are clear signs of the target animal's presence, in the shape of droppings, damage or well-worn narrow paths. It is best to place the trap near a wall, fence, hedge or bank, because animals tend to avoid open spaces when moving from their home to a feeding site. Alternatively, the trap can be placed outside the house or run of vulnerable livestock, such as poultry and fowl. For catching grey squirrels the trap should be placed on flat ground, at the base of a tree that the squirrel frequents; one or two traps will be sufficient to deal with the grey squirrels inhabiting a small woodland. Having selected the best place for the cage trap, the procedure for setting it is as follows:

With either gloves, or hands that have been rubbed in soil to mask human odour, raise the drop door and, depending on the weight of the bait, place it on the treadle plate or at the back of the trap beyond the treadle. Lower the door slightly so that the moving slide rod supports it. Balance the other end of the rod against the treadle hook. Care should be taken to make sure that there is nothing within 15cm of the sliding rod to impinge its movement when the treadle is depressed by the target animal. The trap should be firmly anchored to the ground to prevent it being moved. It can then be covered with long, dry grass and leaves to conceal its outline and make it less obvious, however, this must be put on in such a way as not to interfere with the workings of the trap.

The trap should be inspected at least once a day and I favour checking them in the morning and evening. Rats and grey squirrels cannot, on any account, be released and should be quickly and humanely killed. Shooting the animal in the head with an air rifle is probably the best way of doing this; the dead animal can then be disposed of by burying. In addition to the combination rat/squirrel trap described here, there is also a squirrel cage trap that has a spring-loaded action, which is set in the same way as the rabbit cage trap discussed next. The advantage of this trap is that it will only be triggered by an animal actually entering the trap and placing its weight on the treadle plate, whereas animals from outside the trap can disturb the sliding rod of the rat/squirrel trap.

The Rabbit Cage Trap

The first task in the process of setting the rabbit cage trap is to bait it with something sufficiently tasty to lure the rabbit into the trap. Vegetables are the obvious choice and the small, fresh leaves of brassicas are preferred to the older, larger outer leaves. Rabbits also favour small carrots. The bait should be placed at the rear of the trap, beyond the treadle plate. I usually tie the

Setting a single catch rat trap. The door is raised and bait placed on the treadle plate.

The end of the slide rod being carefully balanced against the treadle hook.

A ferret demonstrating the trap in action.

A multi-catch live trap can be used where there is an abundance of rats. STV INTERNATIONAL

leaves in place on the inside of the rear door and cut small notches into the carrots so that they can be slotted firmly onto the wire at the base of the cage. This makes the rabbit exert itself in order to get the bait, therefore guaranteeing that it will set off the trap. Vegetable bait should not be left protruding through the side or back of the trap, because a crafty rabbit will pull at it from the outside instead of entering the trap.

The common places to site the trap are where there are diggings under a fence or gate, or in the small corridors it creates in the rough ground as it travels from one field to another; along the bottom of hedges or gorse bushes, which it may use as temporary hideaways during the day; and the bolt holes of warrens, if the ground is level enough for the trap to be placed in position.

Once the site has been selected the actual mechanics of setting the live trap are remarkably simple and basically involve the following:

1. Raise the trap door.
2. Engage the setting hook, which in turn will incline the treadle plate.
3. Secure the anchor peg in the ground to prevent movement.

I choose to cover the top and sides of the trap with any vegetation to hand, so that it blends in with the surrounding environment and also provides the caught rabbit with some protection from wet and cold weather. By law the user is obliged to check his trap at least once a day, but I routinely check my rabbit traps first thing in the morning, then at midday and once more in the evening. Best results are achieved when rabbit control measures are carried out during the autumn and winter months; I have also noticed that my largest catches occur when night time temperatures drop to freezing, producing a severe frost.

As rabbits will travel along an assortment of routes when moving from the warren to their feeding site, it is well worth the smallholder having more than one trap, so that he is able to place traps at various points along these paths. This will increase the chances of a catch quite substantially and the number of traps required will depend on the density of the resident rabbit population. However, it should be remembered that the rabbits do not have to be caught all at once. Therefore, between three and six traps should prove sufficient for most situations.

Trapping rabbits is an exercise in patience and the trapper must resist the temptation to move the trap if nothing is caught during the first couple of days. Wild animals can take a long time to lose their suspicion of any changes in their environment; if the trap is moved, the familiarity the rabbits are developing towards the trap will be erased and the whole process will go back to square one. I will leave a trap in the same place for as long as a week; only then, if I have not caught anything, will I change its location.

Bait should be routinely changed at least once every five days, sometimes sooner if field mice pop into the trap and nibble away at some of the vegetables, as they are apt to do without setting off the trap. When a rabbit is found in the trap, the rear door should be opened carefully so that the rabbit can be seized by the loins with one hand. It should then be completely removed from the trap and killed quickly by breaking its neck, either with a chop or the thumb up method. The meat and skin of the rabbit can be kept for household use, while the entrails, offal and head can all be fed to ferrets.

Setting a rabbit trap. With the trap baited with vegetables the spring door is raised and held in position by the setting hook.

With the door open the trap is placed over a rabbit trail.

The anchor rod is driven into the ground to prevent movement.

Long grass is used to camouflage the trap.

Trap with captured rabbit, which has plenty of room in which to move about.

Mink Cage Trap

The mink has powerful jaws and will only be contained by a purpose-built, well-constructed trap made of galvanized weld mesh. Using cage traps to catch mink is the preferred method of water authorities, conservation groups and water bailiffs and achieves a consistent level of success, due to the mink's boldness and curiosity, which makes it an easy animal to trap.

Bait

Although the mink is curious by nature, a fish head should be placed in the trap beyond the treadle plate to ensure that it enters the trap.

Siting and Setting

Because the mink is a water loving animal, the trap should be placed near the ponds, streams or rivers that are in the vicinity of the smallholding. The trap should be placed on flat ground near to the water, preferably at a point where the mink is likely to exit the water. Holes can be dug in a riverbank to contain traps and have the added advantage of arousing the mink's curiosity, as it is a compulsive investigator. As it is a spring-loaded trap, the mink trap is set and works in exactly the same way as the rabbit cage trap.

Dealing With the Catch

Since the mink is an aggressive animal, the best solution is to kill it within the trap. Once again the air rifle is the preferred choice for accomplishing this, by delivering a shot to the head. In most areas throughout the country, initiatives to remove mink from the waterways are being undertaken by conservation groups and river authorities and these bodies offer advice and practical help to anybody troubled by mink.

chapter six

How to Use Rat Poison

SELECTION OF POISON

When choosing a poison, consider the environment in which it is to be used and the diet of the resident rats that you intend to poison. For dry environments, a poison containing whole wheat in grain form may be used, while in damp conditions wax blocks, which are impervious to water and contain a mix of wheat flour, milk protein and chopped wheat, bound by edible waxes are the ideal choice. Rats on a smallholding commonly eat livestock feed containing wheat, oats, peas, maize and linseed; as a result they find wheat-based poison to be palatable, which is essential because the more time the rat spends feasting upon the poison, the more quickly death will occur. The smallholder should always select a poison that contains a bright coloured dye, because this makes any spillage easy to spot and also shows in the rat's droppings and will, therefore, confirm whether the poison is being eaten or not.

STORAGE

Some people who have heard distressing stories of pet dogs dying as a result of consuming rat poison, are understandably wary about using such substances. However, the danger of poison to other animals, whether to pets, livestock or wildlife, not to mention people, can be completely mitigated by actions taken by the smallholder, beginning with adequate storage. The poison should always be kept in a sealed container, which is kept tightly shut when not in use and placed on a shelf that is beyond the reach of children. A dedicated poisons cabinet that can be locked or bolted is preferable. In addition to keeping the poison safe, correct storage will ensure that it remains fresh.

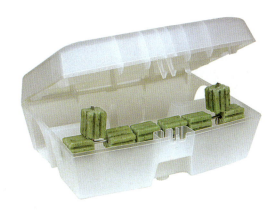

Using rodenticides. Bait blocks should be selected when the poison is to be used in a damp environment.
STV INTERNATIONAL

DISPENSING THE POISON

Where to Place the Poison

Rat poison should never simply be scattered on the ground. Instead it should be put in hoppers or bait stations, which have secure lids. There are an assortment of purpose-built bait stations available made of plastic or metal. Alternatively, they can be home-made utilizing old car tyres, pallets, bricks and slates. These should be constructed so that wildlife, livestock and people cannot come into contact with the poison. After buying ready-made bait stations, I treat them like new traps and expose them to the effects of the weather in order to dull their new look and smell. I then often leave them in the environment where they are most likely to be used for a week or two, so that they become infused with the common smells that a rat is likely to encounter when moving around outside or in the outbuildings and barns. The one and only exception when it is permissible to dispense with a bait station, is when the poison can be placed directly into the holes of rat burrows in a bank or hedge.

The poison should not just be put around the mouth of such holes, but at least 10cm down into them. Consequently, I employ a long-handled spoon so that I can put the poison in a convenient measure, directly where I want it.

Siting of Bait Stations

Just like traps, bait stations should be placed at points along the paths that rats routinely travel to get to their feeding sites. These include: in and around outbuildings, along ditches and hedge bottoms. Bait stations can be placed at 5m intervals for heavy infestations, increasing to 10m when rats are scarce. During the winter months, when rats are most likely to invade a smallholding, it is worth placing some bait stations as a precaution at 15m intervals along the common approaches to the outbuildings, or any other part of the smallholding that is vulnerable to rodent attack.

How Much Bait to Use

This will quite obviously depend upon the number of rats that are present on the

Always place poison in a bait station that can be fastened shut.

The bait station is placed over a rat trail, running alongside the wall of an outbuilding.

smallholding, which is not always easy to estimate accurately. However, it is generally accepted that it is better to be generous with the amount of poison used, because an insufficient amount is recognized as one of the reasons for this method failing to work. Such advice is aimed at the professional pest control operative, who will probably be visiting premises once a week. Unlike them, I am able to inspect the bait stations that I have in use every day; consequently I prefer to start off with just a couple of tablespoons in each bait station. I will then top up and increase the measure in response to how much poison the rats are consuming. Overfilling the stations at the outset can make it difficult during the first few days to determine whether any poison has been taken. When handling bait stations and dispensing poison I favour wearing gloves, because this both protects the user and prevents the transmission of human scent to the stations.

Daily Inspection

Each day the bait stations should be opened to ascertain how much, if any, poison has been consumed and appropriate replenishing undertaken. In conjunction with these daily checks, the ground around the bait stations should be scrutinized to ensure that no poison has been scattered outside the station by feeding rats, which can sometimes happen when they have been filled to capacity. After the first three days, by which time the poison will have reached lethal levels in the rats' bodies, the daily inspection should include looking for any dead or dying animals.

Rats that have been poisoned go through various stages of suffering before they actually die; the final one that precedes death is a complete loss of movement. Consequently, the smallholder may come across motionless rats, in which case he must use an appropriate tool, such as an air rifle, to hasten the animal's death and end its suffering. The smallholder also has an ethical responsibility to do his best to retrieve any rats that have died as a result of the use of rodenticides, in order to prevent the poisoned carcass being consumed by wildlife, which can result in secondary poisoning. Small numbers of poisoned rats may legitimately be buried in a hole at least 30cm in depth.

chapter seven

How to Use Air Rifles on the Smallholding

For those who have no prior knowledge of air rifles and require detailed information regarding their selection and use, I would recommend they refer to specialist books such as *Air Rifle Shooting for Pest Control and Rabbiting* written by my brother and published by the Crowood Press. In the limited space available in this chapter, I will simply offer a basic guideline with a particular emphasis on using an air rifle on the smallholding.

In order to succeed at controlling pests with an air rifle, the smallholder will require the following:

EQUIPMENT

- An air rifle designed for hunting with a power rating of 12ft-lb.

- A telescopic sight. By magnifying the target zone on small mammals to promote a humane kill, the telescopic sight is essential for accurate shooting. It can also be used as an aid for estimating, with reasonable accuracy, the distance from the shooter to the target.
- A torch/lamp that can be fitted to the rifle for shooting in the dark or in low light.
- Hunting pellets which, when matched with the rifle, give consistent results.

KNOWLEDGE

- Lawful use of the air rifle when targeting pests.
- The habits and living environments of pests.
- Which part of the pest's body to aim at to facilitate immediate death. This area is known as the kill zone.
- The workings of the rifle and how different weather conditions may affect shooting.

Modern air rifles are quiet and relatively easy to use, which makes them ideal for use on a smallholding.

SKILLS

Fieldcraft

This refers to the ability to approach pests without scaring them into taking flight and to conceal oneself and remain at a location where pests are active, without being seen.

Marksmanship

The shooter should achieve consistent five-shot, 1in groupings on the target range, before he considers himself ready to pursue live animals.

Range Finding

This is the ability to judge the distance from the shooter to the targeted pest.

Fieldcraft underpins the shooter's efforts because, unless he can get into a position to shoot that is within range, the air rifle simply cannot be used. In order to optimize such skills, the shooter has to acquire a thorough knowledge of the lie of the land, including the barns and outbuildings where he will be using the air rifle, together with the haunts and habits of resident pests. In this respect, smallholders like myself have a clear advantage over visiting pest controllers. This is because I spend so much of my time on the smallholding that I know exactly where to find resident pests and where visiting pests are likely to strike. Furthermore, I am able to identify what time of day they are likely to be most active. Even as I undertake daily chores on the holding, it is not unusual for avian pests to land close by; they tend to ignore my presence because I am such a familiar sight. This means that should they cause damage, I am within shooting range and it does pay dividends to keep an air rifle and pellet

One advantage of the air rifle is that it is suitable for use in and around buildings, which is where the smallholder will do a lot of shooting.

pouch within reach. In such cases the rifle should be unloaded, with the safety catch on when not in use.

The smallholder has two methods of operation to choose from when hunting pests with an air rifle:

The Ambush Technique

To lie in wait at an appropriate location.

Stalking

To pursue an animal by sight and trail.

I shall now briefly identify how these relate to the specific pests that the smallholder is most likely to encounter.

Rabbits

The best time to shoot rabbits is either first thing in the morning or during the evening, because this is typically when they will be above ground, feeding on pasture or among cereal or vegetable crops. The smallholder may pre-empt the rabbits' arrival and lie in wait between the warrens and the feeding site, making use of natural obstacles to camouflage his presence and remaining quiet and still in order to avoid alerting the rabbits. As a rabbit feeds and is stationary it can be shot, making sure to aim at a point on the head between the ear and eye, so that the pellet penetrates the brain.

As an alternative to lying in wait, a shooter may opt to stalk rabbits. This involves patrolling ground that rabbits frequent, spotting them from a distance and then moving within range – approximately 30m

– to shoot the identified target. Stalking is a skill that relies upon making the most of natural features to disguise the shooter's approach and making slow, deliberate movements. Even on those occasions when the stalker is spotted by the targeted rabbit, all may not be lost because a rabbit will sometimes huddle close to the ground, as an alternative to bolting, and remain in such a position for long enough to discharge a shot. Whichever method is used the shot should never be rushed and it is always best to opt for a supported shooting position.

Rats

Unless the smallholder is confronted by a major rodent infestation, the best time to shoot rats is during the evening as darkness descends. The most common place to spot them is around or inside buildings containing livestock, where they search for food remnants. Consequently, rat shooting on the smallholding is most commonly undertaken at ranges as close as 10–20m and a short, light air rifle is best suited to this type of work.

During the winter months, the smallholder may undertake routine searches of his outbuildings with a torch and air rifle and may, occasionally, spot a rat that will remain still long enough for him to shoot it. However, a much more reliable approach is to identify where rats are nesting and feeding, select a suitable hiding place that you can get to before it gets dark and remain in position until the rats appear. For this purpose the air rifle will need to be fitted with a scope-mounted lamp, that has

Camouflage and stealth will be needed to shoot cautious avian pests.

Air rifles are available in different sizes but, for use in confined spaces, the shorter and lighter the air rifle the better.

The smallholder who wants to use an air rifle to pursue rats will require some form of torchlight.

a red filter. This gives a gentle red beam, which is less likely to alarm the rat than a harsh white light. When shooting a rat in these conditions, the red beam should be slowly drifted onto the rat to identify the kill zones, which are from the front between the ears, just above the eyes, or from the side behind the eye.

Feral and Wood Pigeons

The most common places to find feral pigeons are the interior and exterior roof spaces of barns and outbuildings. When my brother was asked by a neighbouring dairy farmer to deal with feral pigeons, he found the greatest concentration of birds was inside large barns, where the pigeons roosted in the rafters and fed on cattle feed remnants. After a couple of days observing the pigeons, he was able to identify the best time of day to shoot, which was when bird numbers were at their optimum, in this case during the early afternoon. Feral pigeons often find their way into an outbuilding through open doors; the simple measure of shutting the door will contain the birds so that they can be shot. They are easily scared and, therefore, the shooter's movements should be quiet and controlled to avoid causing panic. Shooting pigeons that are located in rafters is usually done in the standing position: leaning the back against a wall or pillar is a good way for the shooter to steady his aim. In this environment, the quieter the report of the air rifle, the better. As with rabbits and rats, head shots are recommended.

When wood and feral pigeons descend on cereal and vegetable crops to feed they can be shot. My own observations have revealed that they tend to appear at the same time each day; although they are renowned for their wariness and taking flight, it is not difficult to walk into shooting range, especially when there are hedges and gorse bushes to shield the approach. Alternatively a home-made hide can be constructed, using small square bales near to the feeding sites, in which the shooter can take up position prior to the birds' arrival. Again, an air rifle with a quiet report should be selected, because it is less likely to startle the birds each time a shot is taken. Pigeons commonly spread out when they are feeding and those on the outer limits should be targeted first.

Crows and Magpies

Crows and magpies often have favourite places that they like to frequent on the smallholding, such as the top of fence posts near to poultry sheds, or hovering over the muck heap. Despite at times being quite brazen, these birds like keeping people at a safe distance and seem to have an inbuilt antenna for detecting a person carrying a rifle and rapidly taking flight. Therefore, the smallholder will have to hide himself near to the birds' favourite perching posts in order to get within shooting range, or spy for their presence from the concealment of barn entrances, or from behind bales of straw. When shooting crows or magpies, once again, the head should be aimed at.

Serious hunters will employ a host of decoys and a purpose-built camouflage hide when they are targeting pigeons or crows; however, the average smallholder may not wish to spend money on such items, or invest the amount of time required to use them effectively. Instead, he can take a more leisurely approach to the reduction of bird numbers by spreading what a hunter will hope to achieve in a day over a week, with short, half-hour shooting forays. In some ways this is preferable, because the lengthy periods of waiting for the birds to return to the ground and within shooting range after they have been startled by a shot can be avoided.

Whenever possible, always select a supported shooting position because it will aid accuracy.

chapter eight

Using Dogs to Control Pests

The smallholder of today is ideally situated to continue the tradition of using dogs to control pests, which was established by farmers and cottagers of bygone days. Unlike the professional pest controller's dog, which is a visitor to a customer's land and has a limited amount of time in which to work, the smallholder's dog is a permanent resident, knows the premises intimately and will treat it as its own territory and instinctively want to protect and hunt on it.

However, in order to be of use the dog must be schooled in basic obedience and willingly obey commands to: 'come', 'sit' and 'stay', even when it is excited by the presence of pests, such as rats and rabbits. It is also essential for the dog to prove itself totally trustworthy around livestock, which it must, on no account, bite, chase or harass. This congenial behaviour is achieved through ongoing socialization from an early age and equips the dog with the knowledge to differentiate those animals that are to be treated with respect from the pests. In terms of pest control the

The smallholder's terrier, undergoing essential training.

dog is capable of performing three useful functions. These are as:

1. a deterrent
2. a detector
3. a catcher.

DETERRENT

The dog serves as a pest deterrent by its presence, the noise it makes by barking and its instinct to confront and pursue any intruders, whether these are human or animal. The mere sight of a dog on a smallholding is sufficient to halt pests in their tracks and make them think twice about coming on to the land, or near the buildings where the dog is roaming. The barking of a dog is guaranteed to alert pests to the fact that there is a very real threat in the locality, as a result, they will invariably head for the safety of cover as quickly as possible.

Should the dog actually spot a pest it will give chase and voice, both of which will make the pest take rapid flight. If my terrier gives chase to either a deer or a fox, I will call him back as soon as the animal takes flight, because my intention is simply to scare them away from an area where they can cause damage and not to injure them in any fashion. However, in the case of rabbits and rodents, the terrier is encouraged to continue his pursuit and catch them if he can.

In order to be an effective deterrent, the smallholder should allow his dog to roam about the holding at will, providing that it cannot stray on to other people's land or find its way on to a road, or other such hazardous location. I would also recommend that there is always someone, somewhere on the holding when the dog is at liberty. It is particularly helpful to have a dog that is willing to keep an eye on young stock, whether this is chicks, lambs or goat kids. My Jack Russell is always eager to introduce himself to any new arrivals born on the smallholding and keenly watches them during their early days. He also enjoys playing with lambs and goat kids and I can be confident that nothing will be allowed to harm them while he is acting as playmate and protector.

DETECTOR

There is no doubt that the dog's nose will detect things that the smallholder will not be able to see, such as pests hiding around outbuildings and in hedges. The value of the early detection of pests cannot be over-estimated; it prevents them from having the opportunity to breed or cause

The smallholder's dog must be totally trustworthy around livestock.

The terrier is a habitual searcher for pests.

much damage. Consequently, my terrier is encouraged to accompany me as I undertake the routine tasks that take me into the barns and outbuildings and onto the vegetable plot and pasture land. Never willing to be just an idle spectator, he will inspect every nook, cranny and suspicious hole, in search of pests and he is allowed to investigate any part of the holding he wishes to. If he does not draw my attention to anything I can be fairly confident that pests are not in residence.

When the terrier discovers evidence of a pest's presence he will indicate this by:

- Concentrated scenting of the ground.
- Scratching at the ground or animal bedding within outbuildings.
- Giving voice, ranging from growling to barking.
- Posture and tail wagging.

It is my job to interpret these gestures accurately, so that I can discern if the dog has found a pest, its nest, droppings and feeding site, or simply has scent of it and, therefore, take the appropriate action.

Teaching dogs to detect pests is not difficult, as most breeds possess an instinctive impulse to search anywhere they detect strange smells. This can be further encouraged by taking the dog to a place where you know pests are active and instructing the dog to sniff at the ground, while asking him: 'What have you got?' As soon as the dog begins to scent the area in a systematic fashion and concentrates his efforts on the position where a pest is, or was hiding, or detects and begins to follow the trail that the pest has left, he should be rewarded with praise. After a few sessions the dog will become thoroughly familiar with this type of investigatory work and will have its senses trained to pick up the slightest whiff of pests.

If the smallholder is going to use the dog in this way, he will have to know how to act promptly and decisively when the dog does find pests. I have learnt with my terrier that there are basically three options; deciding which to take will depend upon the type and density of cover the pest has, and what the chances of the dog actually making a catch are. The options are:

1. Allow the dog to get on with the task without interfering and just observe his progress; either because the pest is so well covered there is nothing a person can do to help, or because disturbing the dog may give the pest the chance to escape.

2. Assist the dog in his efforts. This includes: removal of obstacles, enabling the dog to get at the pest, blocking a pest's escape route to prevent it evading the dog, and using ferrets to drive the pest into the path of the dog.

3. Call the dog off. This is done when an alternative method is more likely to achieve the desired results, in which case the dog should be called off, before it disturbs the pest to such a degree that it bolts before the smallholder has the chance to implement his chosen method.

CATCHING PESTS

During my late grandfather's era, whenever a rat was spotted on a farm, or in a garden, the first response was to call for the nearest terrier. This highlights the reputation the terrier has earned itself as the supreme vermin catcher. It is a reputation that dates back centuries and has been validated again and again by countless successful displays of rat and rabbit catching. The combination of instinct, small athletic physique, many generations of working blood and legendary tenacity, is what makes the terrier such an unrelenting and accomplished catcher of pests. Of course there are other breeds that have a lot to offer in this respect and chief among them are lurchers, whippets and collies. However, for the smallholding environment, which has a variety of outbuildings, hedges and gorse bushes, in my opinion, the terrier cannot be bettered. Consequently, in respect of catching pests, the characteristics displayed by the typical working terrier will serve as a model. These include:

No hole or digging escapes the scrutiny of my terrier.

Curiosity

It has been said that my Jack Russell is always looking for trouble. Although this may be considered a little disparaging, it highlights the fact that he possesses a lively interest in his surroundings and all that is going on around him. This manifests itself, for example, with him searching around the poultry shed, and even disappearing under it, each time I let the chickens out. This constant being on the lookout is the hallmark of a successful pest control dog and is quite easy to encourage, simply by giving the dog the time and opportunity to indulge his instincts, as well as offering verbal prompts and praise.

Alert Senses

While the searching of outbuildings and hedgerows is born of curiosity, it is the information gathered by alert senses, chiefly smell, but also sight and hearing, that enable the terrier to catch the fleeting movement of a rodent, hear the squeaking of mice or the stamping of rabbits' feet, that alerts the dog to the nearby presence of a pest. Such senses are instinctive and heightened by experience.

Quick Reactions

Whether the pest that the dog has discovered is a rat, rabbit or even a mouse, there is no time to waste before taking

action. Even a momentary delay can result in the pest escaping. The dog must move in on the pest at speed. This is best undertaken by the dog using its own initiative, because interference by the handler can result in the dog becoming overexcited or confused, leading to a lapse in its concentration, which is all the pest will require to make good its escape.

A Powerful Bite

With the pest cornered or trapped, the dog must act decisively and seize hold of it firmly in its mouth and deliver a lethal blow, by tightening its powerful, vice-like jaws in one deliberate movement. Dogs that want to retrieve the live animal to give to the handler, or maul the pest without first killing it, are not suitable for this particular aspect of canine pest control; they could get injured by the pest, especially when dealing with rodents, as well as cause unnecessary distress and suffering to the pest. Having killed a pest, the dog should drop it instantly and then check for further pests. Any inclination the dog has to either consume, or run off with the dead animal, should be firmly dealt with.

The only assistance I offer to my terrier when he is attempting to catch a pest is to:

- Remove any obstacle or debris that is preventing the dog getting to the pest.
- Block or guard any potential exits to prevent the pest escaping from the dog.

Although I resist the temptation to interfere when my terrier is pursuing pests, I will allow and even encourage my brother's collie to assist the terrier. This is because they have worked together when ferreting and are an accomplished team, knowing precisely how to complement one another.

I also purposefully take him to locations where pests are likely to be found, such as the hedged boundary of the pasture in the morning and evening, when rabbits are feeding, or when mucking out the deep litter beds from the goat barn, which can result in the unearthing of pests, mainly mice. In such cases the terrier is often able to catch and kill the pests. On the smallholding, my Jack Russell terrier has caught numerous rats, rabbits and mice, a hare and a stray ferret that was making its way towards the hen house. These are the only pests that I allow my terrier to pursue, with the prospect of actually catching and killing them.

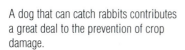
A dog that can catch rabbits contributes a great deal to the prevention of crop damage.

chapter nine

How to Use Ferrets to Control Pests

I first encountered ferrets when my brother procured two albinos from the local gamekeeper and, with his usual optimism, claimed that they would soon put an end to the rats that seemed determined to construct a home under our chicken shed. Nearly three decades have elapsed since then, during which time we have always kept a number of ferrets, utilizing their innate fierce hunting skills to catch rabbits throughout the winter months, in order to both minimize crop damage and have a healthy, free, meat supply to complement our home-grown vegetables. The ferrets are also constantly on hand to deal with any rats that attempt to hide in, or under, any of our outbuildings. Using ferrets is a traditional and straightforward way to deal effectively with such pests and entire books have been written on the subject. However, I shall confine my comments to outlining the basic procedures for using ferrets in conjunction with purse nets, to catch rabbits, and describe how I have used them to flush rats from their hiding places.

RABBIT CATCHING

In order to catch rabbits the smallholder will require the following:

- A healthy well-handled ferret.
- A selection of purse nets, ranging in length from 100–150cm. Hand-made nets of either 7 ply hemp or 6z spun nylon, are the nicest and easiest to use. Alternatively, machine-made nets of 10z nylon can be used. Tapering wooden net pegs, approximately 18cm long must be attached to the braided draw cord of each purse net.
- A carrying box for transporting the ferret to the warren. These can be made of 11mm OSB board, with typical dimensions being 35cm long and 25cm wide and high. It should have holes for ventilation, a strap so that it can be carried over the shoulder and a lid that can be shut securely.
- A game bag or rucksack to carry the nets in.
- A small clip point knife for legging dead rabbits so that they can be easily transported.

Using ferrets to catch rabbits takes place during daylight hours, generally from late September to early March. Although I have ferreted in every type of winter weather, strong wind and snowfall can make it difficult to set nets, while constant rain can make it hard keeping on your feet when

This shows a vast array of ferreting equipment; however, a selection of purse nets, a ferret and something to carry it in will suffice to get started.

working warrens near a stream, as the ground becomes increasingly muddy.

Ferreting is a process that is centred on the rabbit warren and a smallholder should be able to pinpoint exactly where these are on his land. One of the first things that I did when I moved into my present smallholding, was to explore every inch of ground and have a good root around gorse bushes, along hedges and in ditches, in search of any resident wildlife, such as rabbits, so that I would be able to keep an eye on their proliferation and activity. As a result I know precisely where rabbits are to be found on my land and, with a fair degree of accuracy, even how many there are.

Catching rabbits with ferrets is a simple, straightforward process that involves the following:

Warren Inspection

Time spent carefully surveying the warren, so that each and every bolt hole is identified, is crucial to achieving success. As well as the obvious holes, look for the well concealed bolt holes that can be as much as 3m away from the main warren. They can be difficult to find because, having been dug from the inside, there are no tell-tale mounds of earth to highlight them and there is often long grass growing over them. It pays to have a good poke about with a stick in the rough ground around a warren to make sure that no holes have been missed.

Net Setting

Place a purse net of the appropriate size by each of the holes of the warren. Unravel the net and secure the peg, up to three quarters of its length, into the ground. If this cannot be done with hand pressure, you should employ a mallet with a rubber striker to drive the peg in. Taking hold of the top and bottom rings in either hand, stretch the net over the middle of the hole and then pull the edges of the net in opposite directions, until the net is roughly circular in shape, with the entire circumference of it resting on the ground bordering the hole. Care should be taken to ensure that the net does not sag back into the hole and that there are no small gaps left around the edges, where it should be in contact with the ground. This process should be

repeated until all the holes of the warren are properly covered.

Entering the Ferret

This refers to the deployment of the ferret into the warren. The experienced ferreter will cast his eye over the entire warren and select, what he believes to be, the best hole to enter or release the ferret into. Typically this will be the lowest point of the warren when it is located on a slope, the end hole of a warren that occurs in a straight line at the base of a hedge, and the hole nearest to a tree or bush when working a warren that is spread around the trunk of a tree, or linked in with sprawling gorse bushes.

To release the ferret correctly, hold the animal around the belly with its paws resting on the ground, lift the bottom of the net and place the ferret, with its nose facing forward, directly into the mouth of the hole, so that it can simply walk off your hand into the warren. Once the ferret is out of sight, replace the net and stand well back so that you can keep an eye on all of the nets that have been set in anticipation of a rabbit bolting.

Anybody who uses ferrets on a regular basis to catch rabbits, quickly learns that he has to be patient and stand quietly while the ferret goes about its subterranean

Ferret being entered to a rabbit warren.

work. Sometimes it seems to take just a few moments for the rabbits to bolt, while at other times it may take at least half an hour. Whichever is the case, as soon as the rabbit hits the net it should be seized by the loins and dispatched immediately, while still in the net, using the chin up or chop method. As soon as this is done, place the rabbit well out of the way and put another purse net over the hole that the rabbit bolted from. Wait for the process to be repeated until the ferret has emptied the warren and reappeared above ground; it can then be retrieved and returned to the carrying box for a well-earned rest. The nets can then be gathered before you turn your attention to the dead rabbits. These should be:

1. Disentangled from the nets that have pursed around them.
2. The bladder should be forcibly emptied by placing the thumb of one hand on the lower part of the abdomen and then moving it downward, towards the tail, with firm pressure applied throughout the movement.
3. Legged so that they can be easily carried. This involves threading one hind leg of the rabbit through the other, by means of a vertical 2cm cut made just above the hock.
4. Tied or placed on a stick so that they can be carried home, where they can be skinned and butchered.

RAT CATCHING

Although ferrets have been employed in the past with some success to chase rats from their burrows into purpose-made nets, I prefer to limit the use of my ferrets to the following two methods, which I feel minimizes the risk of injury to the ferret from these fierce antagonists.

Flushing Rats from their Hiding Places

I remember one occasion when I was sitting in the pig shed, rubbing the belly of Primrose, a gargantuan Oxford Sandy and Black sow, spotting the fleeting movements of some small creatures through a crack in the wooden floor. It did not take me long to realize that these were rats and I was not surprised because pig arcs, poultry houses, sheds, stables and garages are buildings which brown rats have always had a tendency to live under.

The traditional response was to enter a burly hob to flush the rats out. Clearly this would have been pointless unless suitable preparations had been made for dealing with the rats as they emerged from their cover. During my late grandfather's era this included gathering all his male neighbours together, arming them with large shovels and positioning them strategically so that the entire building was surrounded. They

The ferret is an instinctive burrow hunter.

were tasked with striking a fatal blow to the bolting rats, which takes a remarkable amount of speed and precision. A better option for those of us today who do not have either such speed, or the level of manpower, is to erect some form of barrier around the building. Wooden boards 100cm high or straw bales placed two high can be utilized for this purpose. The intention of this is to momentarily disorientate and trap any fleeing rats, so that a waiting team of terriers can pounce on them with relative ease.

The job of the ferret is simply to drive the rats from under the buildings. None of my ferrets has ever showed any fear of rats or hesitation about disappearing under floors to chase them from their hiding place. Typically, having a variety of exit holes, the rats will escape from the ferret with relative ease; when a number of them are present they will bolt in a variety of different directions at the same time, which is why it is so important to place a barrier that surrounds the entire building.

Obviously, if rats are resident under sheds containing poultry and fowl, the birds will need to be shut up securely in their houses or moved to a safe place before the ferret can be released, in order to avoid it getting sidetracked and chasing or attacking any of the birds. As well as protecting livestock from the ferret, there are some situations, such as the one involving my Oxford Sandy and Black pigs, when the smallholder will need to protect his ferret from large animals that may, in the excitement, unintentionally harm the ferret. Furthermore, it is also very difficult to concentrate on dealing with rats when a curious pig that appears to have the strength of three men in its snout, is intent on cajoling you into a game by repeatedly thrusting your wellington boots in the air. Therefore, I always take the time to prepare a safe working environment for my ferret and terrier, which ensures that they will not trouble or be troubled by livestock. When undertaken correctly this is one of the quickest ways to eradicate rats.

Pursuing Cornered Rats

During the winter months of the year, when rats are most likely to invade a smallholding, I routinely inspect my buildings inside and out in the evening as the daylight gives way to darkness; on numerous occasions, with the aid of torchlight, I have spotted rats going about their business. Sometimes they have scampered off at incredible speed and all I was able to do was carefully note the route they travelled along so that I could take appropriate measures, such as setting a trap for the following night.

At other times my presence and the quick reactions of my Jack Russell have prevented the rat following its chosen route and forced it to flee for the nearest obstacle that will provide it with cover. These have included: behind water barrels, in between the gaps of badly stacked logs, underneath pallets and behind storage cupboards or cages in outbuildings. Pursuing the rat with my dog resulted in the animal being trapped but beyond reach of the terrier, irrespective of how far he brazenly forced his snout into the small space where the rat was hiding. In such situations I have found that the best thing to do is to leave the dog in position to prevent the rat escaping while I get a ferret, usually a large hob, to assist in the rat hunt.

Ferrets are tremendous contortionists and can fit into the tight spaces that a rat will find to hide in, which are out of reach of the dog. All I have to do is place my ferret on the floor where I last saw the rat and he does the rest, quickly entering the tiny hiding place where the rat is confined. In a one-on-one confrontation, the ferret definitely has the supremacy, even over large healthy rats. Usually within moments of releasing my hob I will hear a loud screech, after which my ferret returns completely unperturbed leaving a dead rat in his wake. With his work done the ferret is returned to his cage so that I can turn my attention to retrieving and correctly disposing of the rat.

LEFT: Even when livestock is well mannered, like this pig, it should be contained elsewhere if the ferret is going to be used to search for rabbits under and around the pig house.

RIGHT: Ferrets make relentless and fierce pursuers of rodents. This jill displayed a particular talent for unearthing rats.

chapter ten

How to Use Electric Fencing for Pest Control

The smallholder can use electric fencing to prevent damage to crops from rabbits, hares and deer and to protect livestock from predatory animals. There are two types of electric fencing suitable for these purposes and these are classified as: netting and wire strands respectively, which we shall now look at in turn.

HOW TO PUT UP ELECTRIC NETTING

Electric netting is a great favourite amongst smallholders because it can be used for a variety of purposes, including strip grazing and moveable poultry runs. It is also extremely easy to set, because it has integral posts at approximately 3m intervals. There are also kits available for: poultry, goats, sheep or rabbits, which are generally 50m in length and incorporate a suitable energizer, earth stake and four corner posts. The difference between the netting for these various animals is the height of the fence and the size of the square meshes. Typically poultry netting is 110cm high with meshes 7cm wide and 5cm high at the base, ranging to 20cm at the top, whereas rabbit netting is between 50 and 75cm high. A lot of smallholders in the past have purchased poultry netting, which

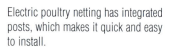

Electric poultry netting has integrated posts, which makes it quick and easy to install.

they have also used successfully to protect crops from rabbits. The advantage of this is that they were able to use the netting to mark the boundaries of moveable poultry runs, once the crops were out of danger or harvested.

The process of putting netting up is straightforward and is as follows:

1. Measure the length of fencing required by striding out the distance, bearing in mind that netting does not have to be placed in a square to work. If required it can be placed in a straight line and easily adapts to the contours of the land.
2. Trim any rough grass that is sticking up where the fence is to be placed.
3. Unravel the netting, letting it rest on the ground as you go.
4. Go back to the beginning and push the first post into the ground. Walk along the fence, pushing each of the posts into the ground in turn. Before pushing a post into the ground, it should be pulled, with just enough force to take up the slack from the preceding stretch of netting. A corner post should be put in place when there is a sharp change of direction.
5. Push the earth stake into the ground at the beginning of the fence.
6. Attach leads from the energizer to the earth stake and fence.
7. Place a warning sign on the fence and switch the energizer on.

It is recommended that rabbit netting be placed at a 70 degree angle, so that it will prevent rabbits jumping over it, or getting close enough to the base to tunnel underneath the fence without being shocked. Should an area greater than 50m need fencing, successive stretches of netting can easily be clipped together.

HOW TO PUT UP ELECTRIC WIRE FENCING

Wire strands tend to be preferred for protecting livestock from foxes and crops from deer, as it is considered more suitable than netting for fencing long lengths and large areas, measuring hundreds of metres. For ease of use, wire can be purchased already wound onto reels, which can be fastened to purpose-made reel posts. The process for setting up a fence using wire strands is as follows:

1. Ascertain the amount of wire and number of posts required, by roughly measuring the area to be fenced. Bear in mind that the figure for the wire will need multiplying by the number of strands that are required, to deter the pest in question. The general recommendations for the number of wire strands are as follows:

   - rabbit   4–6 strands
   - fox   8 strands
   - deer   4 strands
   - muntjac   5 strands
   - badger   4 strands

   As for the posts, one is placed every 5–6m.
2. Insert a reel post into the ground at the beginning of the length to be fenced and place the appropriate number of reels on the post, remembering that one reel will be required for each strand of wire.
3. Push an anchor post into the ground and then a succession of multiwire posts, sufficient to cover the designated area. Multiwire posts are made of plastic and range in height from 100–150cm, with the taller ones being used for fencing aimed at keeping out

Electric wire strands being used to contain a powerful pig. It is equally effective at keeping out pests such as foxes, badgers and deer.

deer and foxes. Wherever there is a sharp change of direction, a corner post should be installed, and an anchor or end post containing insulators should be placed where the fence terminates.

4. Secure the reels to the reel post and feed the respective strands of wire through each of the multiwire posts, at the appropriate height for the animals the fence is to control. Pull the strands of wire hand tight as you go, so that it does not sag; after the wire has been secured to the end post, lock the reels in position in order to maintain the tension. Over two decades ago when I first used electric fencing, I knew some farmers who would simply tie the strands to the beginning and end post and, when they wanted to move it, would wrap each strand of wire around the anchor post. Although these worked adequately, the inclusion of reels makes the task of moving and maintaining the fence much easier.

5. Insert earth stake into the ground at the beginning of the fence, attach an appropriate energizer and place

warning signs on the fence to inform people that it is operative.

By erecting a rabbit fence at an angle of 70 degrees, it will prevent the rabbits getting close enough to the base of the fence to burrow under it without getting shocked. When establishing a semi-permanent or permanent electric fence, different posts from the ones used for the temporary fencing discussed above are required. In such cases, metal or wooden posts should be used, with insulators attached, through which the wire is threaded. Tensioners are also incorporated on each strand to facilitate easy maintenance.

Post showing holders set at different heights for strands of electric wire.

chapter eleven

Using Deterrents, Repellents and Bird Scarers

DEER AND WILDLIFE DETERRENT

There are a variety of devices available that use light and sound to scare a pest away from an area where it can cause damage to crops and set back the hard work of the smallholder. Most of these share common features and are popular because they are non-lethal and, more importantly, are triggered by the pests themselves as they approach the deterrent. In order to make use of a deterrent the following steps should be undertaken:

- Select the trees, crops or livestock that are to be guarded with the deterrent.
- Identify the paths that the targeted pests will travel along to get at the crops.
- Locate a position that overlooks these paths and fasten the deterrent to a fencepost, wall, structure or tree. In the absence of any such features, a fencepost can be driven into the ground and left in place for as long as the deterrent is needed. Where only small areas are concerned, i.e. less than 8m,

the deterrent can be positioned so that its PIR range overlooks the entire area, the result being that a pest within the designated area will constantly trigger the device providing a strong impetus for it to move on.

- Adjust the controls on the deterrent to the desired settings. These include the duration of time the deterrent remains on for after being triggered, the coverage area of the PIR motion detector and the volume of the radio station that the deterrent is tuned in to. These should be experimented with to achieve best results, personally I prefer to have a duration time of around thirty seconds and a volume that is equivalent to that generated by the human voice in normal conversation.
- The deterrent should be turned off at those times of the day when pest activity is absent and should be moved completely once the threat of pest damage is over.
- Deterrents can be fixed to barns and sheds containing poultry and fowl to scare off predators during the night;

Controls and power source of wildlife deterrent.

Wildlife deterrents can be fixed to trees or, as in this case, fence posts.

however, these will be more effective in rural areas where the wildlife are much more wary of human noises and light than their urban relatives.

REPELLENTS

These are of limited use to the smallholder because of the large areas of land and size of crops he deals with, compared to the average gardener who such products are chiefly aimed at. Nevertheless they can be employed effectively when they are limited to small areas to prevent damage to seedlings and young plants, or to support other methods of control. Their primary use is to tackle crop-eating and pasture-damaging pests such as: rabbits, deer, grey squirrels and moles.

Generally, repellents are placed directly on to the crops, trees or pasture where the pests are active. The manufacturer's recommendations should be adhered to regarding application. With the exception of mole granules, the wildlife and squirrel repellents are in liquid form and can be dispensed by means of a watering can or sprayer. They should be dispensed when the weather gives them time to dry thoroughly, after which they should not be unduly affected by rainfall. Mole granules are scattered on the ground surrounding mole hills. Once in position the granules may be watered to hasten the release of the castor oil component, which taints the mole's food source as it filters down into the tunnels. Reapplication of repellents is usually undertaken every forty-eight hours until pest damage is eradicated.

Repellents are commonly available in granule and powder form and are scattered, or made into a liquid and sprayed on the ground.

Modern bird scarers should be pushed firmly into the ground so that they can withstand the force of the wind.

BIRD SCARERS

In order to achieve the desired results, bird scarers must be positioned in the midst of the fruit, vegetable or cereal crops that are susceptible to damage. One bird scarer is required for every 200m and it should be installed before seeding or fruit ripening occurs, to prevent feeding habits becoming established. A bird scarer must be secured firmly in the ground or attached to a post, so that it can withstand windy weather. I favour placing bird scarers at various heights, in a deliberately haphazard fashion and swapping them about every couple of days to prevent birds growing accustomed to and, subsequently, ignoring them.

Home-made scarecrows can be made in the traditional style, using old clothes stuffed with straw. To be effective, such a scarecrow needs to realistically resemble the human figure and should be adorned with some bright reflective clothing. As the idea of the scarecrow is to mimic a person it should be moved about the plot on a daily basis.

A selection of old clothes suitable for making a scarecrow.

Straw is used to make the main body of the scarecrow and give it shape.

The finished scarecrow is arranged so that it looks like a person tending the vegetable plot.

chapter twelve

Feed Bins and Poultry Feeders

Feed bins are used to make the process of feeding livestock easier, by enabling a supply of the relevant feed to be kept, either in the same outbuildings as the animals it is intended for, or in a nearby storage shed conveniently situated for the preparation and distribution of feeds. The bins are vital as they deny pests access to the valuable feeds and, in the process, prevent it from being stolen or fouled which would render it unusable. Metal bins are the preferred choice, but good quality ones can be difficult to find and are expensive. However, they are impregnable to pests and will last for many decades. I have also used thick moulded plastic bins and, despite the fact that a determined rat could eventually gnaw a hole in them, I have never had a bin damaged by rodents and they have proved adequate for protecting feeds. Irrespective of the type of bins used, the lids should always be held securely in place by a handle or weighted object to ensure that, if an animal unexpectedly escapes from its stall when no one is present, it will be unable to gorge itself on the contents of the bin which can adversely affect the sensitive digestive systems of livestock.

Poultry feeders are in many respects like small feed bins, with the exception that they are accessed by the chickens on demand. A bird will require time to develop the habit of using these feeders because they incorporate a variety of settings for the pivoting lid. To start with the lid is left open, so that the birds can get used to feeding while standing on the platform. After a week the setting is changed, so that the lid lies closer to the feeding trough and the platform is raised 25mm off the floor. The sight of food and their familiarity with the

A bin which features a fastening lid that makes it suitable for the storage of animal feed. DOMESTIC FOWL TRUST

The lid of this automatic feeder is secured in the open position while the chicken gets used to it.

BELOW: Feeder in the closed position, showing the raised platform which the chickens have learnt to stand on to lift the lid, so that they can access the food contained in the trough.

platform will encourage the birds to step onto it, which correspondingly raises the lid, giving access to the layers' pellets. After a week of the chickens feeding in this manner, the final adjustment is made so that the lid closes completely over the feeding trough. By now the chickens are fully aware of where the pellets are contained and have come to associate standing on the inclined platform with raising the lid so that food can be eaten. Not only does this feeding system offer no incentive or opportunity to pests, it also prevents the chickens themselves from wasting any pellets. It is suitable for use both within chicken sheds and outside.

chapter thirteen

Protecting Crops and Trees

POLYTUNNELS

Gardening books and polytunnel manufacturers provide detailed information regarding how to site and erect a polytunnel; I have therefore decided to confine my comments to points that deal with integrating the management of the polytunnel into the running of the smallholding. In conjunction with being placed in the best position to benefit from solar heat and light, the polytunnel should be put in a location that:

- Is easy to get to so that the smallholder is not deterred from going to tend it during bad weather, which is when its produce is of vital importance due to the limited quantity of vegetable crops that will grow outside throughout the winter months.
- Has water nearby. A smallholding with an assortment of barns and outbuildings is ideally suited to rainwater harvesting; this should be of sufficient volume to irrigate the polytunnel throughout the year. Water can be pumped from butts around the outbuildings to a storage tank that has been put close to the polytunnel. Alternatively, jerry cans filled with water can be loaded onto a trailer and then driven to the storage tank. The

ongoing task of watering a polytunnel for maximum vegetable production, should not be underestimated and a well thought out irrigation system is essential.

Cloches should be made so that they are easy to move and the inclusion of a lifting lid makes watering easy.

- Is easy to get to from the muck heap. The soil within a polytunnel can soon become exhausted, unless it is nourished by digging in generous amounts of well-rotted manure each year. A correctly managed muck heap will produce the required amounts of such manure and a polytunnel should be situated in a position that makes the task of moving muck to it less demanding, particularly as many smallholders may not have large tractors to do the hard work for them.

CLOCHES

While cloches are typically seen as a way to extend the growing season, they can also prove to be an effective way to keep pests, especially birds and deer, off vegetable crops. Cloches can be made cheaply out of scrap wood, stripped from pallets, and horticultural clear plastic, to any dimensions that are required. The ones that I make have lifting lids to aid ventilation and to allow rain to water the crops, so that there is not the same need for water as there is with the polytunnel. These lids are simply closed or left only slightly open during the times of day when deer may pose a problem, or when birds are hovering overhead. Make or buy cloches that can withstand weather damage, principally caused by the wind, and that can be easily moved from one part of the holding to another.

HORTICULTURAL NETTING

Covering fruit and vegetables with netting is an obvious way to stop avian and mammalian pests spoiling valuable produce. However, simply laying netting over the top of plants is not going to be very effective, as little beaks and mouths can easily push their way through loose netting. At the very least, the netting should be taut to make a distance of 10–20cm between it and the crops. The netting should be put on in such a way to make it easy to roll back to gain access to weed the crops; it will also have to be anchored to the ground to prevent small animals burrowing under it. Horticultural netting can be stretched over purpose-made wooden frames, which are either small enough to lift off the plants when weeding is required, or have lids that can be opened to gain access to the crops.

FRUIT CAGE

For fruit that has a permanent place on the smallholding and is not rotated like vegetable crops, a fruit cage that is tall enough to walk under, is the obvious way to prevent pests stealing fruit. These can be expensive but good ones are built to last and prove an effective way of protecting fruit, which the grower can rely on. It is possible to make your own version using lengths of timber 48mm by 48mm thick and covering it with horticultural netting. Whether bought or home-made, the cage should be checked regularly for any damage, especially following snowfall or strong winds, so that prompt repairs can be made. In areas where there is a high annual snowfall, it may be worth incorporating additional overhead supports in order to prevent the netting sagging excessively, or being torn by the weight of the snow. Fruit cages are only suitable for small to medium-sized fruit patches, chiefly because of cost; as a result the fruit garden on a smallholding will have to be carefully planned. Large fruit patches will have to rely on pest control measures that do not require the covering of the entire plot.

TREE GUARDS

In order to make the best use of tree guards, first identify the trees that will require the protection offered by these simple and straightforward items. Animals or birds do not often damage mature, established trees, however, young and newly planted trees are vulnerable and can be killed outright if the tender growing shoots are eaten. When planting trees, bear in mind that harsh weather and snow-covered ground will mean that they will probably be the easiest source of much-needed food for animals, such as rabbits. They will consume any green growth and strip the bark to get at the soft green bast tissue. Some trees may survive this treatment, but can take years to recover.

Secondly, select an appropriate guard. Those required for deterring rabbits do not need to be as high or robust as those used to combat damage caused by deer, which browse to a height of 2m. Home-made tree guards are simple to make: chicken wire pressed into a cylindrical shape and attached to a post with cable ties will be sufficient to deter rabbits. In the case of deer, weld mesh or stockproof fencing will be required to make the guard, which should be held in place by two or three posts.

A tree guard must be tied to a stake, which has been driven into the ground.

Index